"This honest, candid book has been
a long time coming."

"I read your book four times and it
has changed my life."

"Thanks to this book, I am having
regular sex for the first time."

What the HELL do Women *really* Want ?

SECOND EDITION

ISLAND
FLOWER
BOOKS

Dr. Jama Clark

Published by Island Flower Books
P.O.Box 472157
San Francisco, CA   94147-2157 U.S.A.
1-800-BOOKS-41

Copyright ©1997, completely revised

First Printing 1994

ISBN: 0-9642254-1-7

$22.95

Disclaimer: The purpose of this book is to educate and to give an overview of men's and
women's relationship problems. The author and Island Flower Books shall have neither liability nor responsibility to any person or entity with respect to any loss or damage caused or
alleged to be caused, directly or indirectly by the information in this book. If you are experiencing any kind of psychological or physiological problems as a result of your interpersonal
relationships, you should see a medical doctor, or a licensed clinician to be assessed. The
advice in this book should not be construed to be all of the information which is needed to
make a educated evaluation of social anxiety.

For Annie

ACKNOWLEDGMENTS

The author would like to thank Marnie Sunderbruch for her sunshine and her editing; Mr. James Flood Bailey for his hospitality and endurance; Rebecca, my wonderful, patient designer; David Allen for his help in time of need; Jon Irvin for his spiritual guidance; David Stover for the meaningful passages; Lou and Bill for their mentoring; Dr. David Buss for his research; Susan Clark and Dr. Haines Ely for their contributions; all my clients and friends in Seattle for supporting my research, and my mother for the female energy I appreciate and cherish.

Table of Contents

"O' she doth teach the torches to burn bright."

—*Shakespeare*

Foreword

This book is not about changing the world, the patterns of society, or even women. As frustrating as they are, let's face it, gentlemen, you want them. This book is about how to get and keep attractive women in your life. Enjoying a little physical affection wouldn't be a bad idea either, would it?

Millions of females want you to know what they want so they can get closer to you. However, in their quest to tell you these things, they get cranky, pushy, overly blunt, and may even resort to ACTING UNLADYLIKE to get their point across. They'd get specific, but they don't want to offend you more than they already have.They'd rather "just be friends" than tell you that you are acting like, shall we say- a doormat? In any case, certainly not the kind of man they had hoped for.

After lecturing to thousands of men and asking questions that couldn't be answered in a textbook, I discovered that no one was really telling men the truth about what women wanted, that women don't want men who are timid. No one was explaining a woman's desire for a man to act assertive from a female point of view! This is the dirty, socially unacceptable, politically improper stuff that women complain about constantly over coffee with their friends. In my travels, I met many men who were perplexed, frustrated, and lonely. They didn't understand what women wanted, and I wasn't sure I knew either!

So, I asked questions in my own relationship. What was I doing that was driving him nuts? What was he doing that caused me to react the way I did? I noticed for example, that the more I demanded of him, the less he wanted to give me. When I appreciated him for who he was, and not who I wanted him to be, he was more willing to give back. And when he stopped letting me tell him what to do, I loved it. Suddenly, I started noticing how women bad-mouthed men. How could they ever allow men to care for them with such negative attitudes? No wonder men weren't offering commitments! I am not condoning or implying that women should stop asking for what they want or act weak. However, it's completely possible to be both a powerful and a feminine woman. A real feminist can appreciate male energy without denigrating it.

The more men give their power away the more women complain, for no woman respects a man she can step on. It was time to start teaching these things to men. So I began offering seminars to men, explaining what was going on in the female mind and body.

This book is the outgrowth of those seminars. It's about how to avoid being mistreated by women. It's about learning what women *do* want from a woman's point of view. It contains facts that most women don't tell men, a kind of "woman's locker room" tell-all behind closed doors. Sorry guys, but this book will *not* tell you what the heck is wrong with women for wanting the type of male behavior I'm about to describe. What it does teach you is *why* they want what they want. Some of these things may frustrate you; I'm sorry to break the news, but I hope that the truth will give you less grief so you won't have your money and your time wasted over and over again. (May you never be LJBF'd—"*Let's just be friends'd*"—ever again.)

The first version of this book received positive reactions from all over the country. Men were relieved to hear the truth and reported that women were much happier to have them around when they were direct and assertive. Men who had never been kissed before started getting girlfriends. Men who had girlfriends started having satisfying sexual lives when they stopped allowing themselves to be pushed around. Their work lives improved with their renewed self-esteem. And over ninety percent of the woman who read my book agreed with most of the major points.

I had not anticipated that even the small, simple truths were not being taught. Dress up, use manners, make sure her car starts first before you drive off. Don't fawn over her. During my lectures, I remembered the little things that my dates had done to please me that I had taken for granted. Bringing me one flower, opening the door, the courtship that was sadly disappearing with the younger generation—behavior that I never studied in a social science journal. Worried that maybe this chivalry was becoming less important to younger women, that assertive behavior might be less desired by women in their twenties, I asked. Do you still like it when he asks you out? How do you feel when he doesn't pay? Do like having him make a pass at you after two dates?

And I asked the twenty-eight year old guys, "Was it cool to cry when you skinned your knee when you were a little boy?" The answer, sadly, is still no. And women continue to complain that men don't talk about their feelings! Confused by the messages sent out in the seventies and eighties, men pulled back their power attempting to please us, and got kicked in the teeth. This book explains why.

I am going to describe behaviors that more than ninety percent of the women I have worked with in research studies, classes, and seminars all over the United States say they want in a man. Much of this information has also been documented by international research teams. For you scientific types who want more evidence to prove that these behaviors work, I've listed several excellent references at the back of the book that explain the theoretical and anthropological data concerning male and female mating tendencies.

What's important for you to know is that these techniques are not some sort of self-help, fly-by-night, *Letterman's-Top-Ten-List* of how to get laid. (However, I can certainly tell you that the information in this book will get you there faster.) The methods I outline here are absolutely going to work, <u>if you work them</u>. Every man who tried these techniques came back successful. There <u>are</u> answers to the female craziness you have been experiencing.

While writing my dissertation concerning the dating behavior of single women, I read all of the research I could get my hands on concerning what both sexes wanted in a mate. I studied countless professional journals, and reams of literature about body language, self-esteem, social anthropology, and sexual attraction. I'd like to point out that most graduate schools do not accept dissertation research entitled, *"An Analysis of the Human Female's Reaction to French Kissing"* or *"The Effect of Classy Shoes on the White Collar Woman"*. But, considering how little practical information is available about dating for men, these topics would be gladly received.

Science confirmed what I had intuitively known all along: Most men prefer slender women with longer hair who are young and pretty. This, of course is not a big deal to you because you already know that. What was of interest to me was the ancient reasoning behind these simple truths, which has continued to unconsciously trigger men through the centuries. A woman's shape is important to a man because she is wired for producing babies. Her hair, waist, and youth cause him to be attracted to her because these characteristics indicate she's likely to be more *fertile*. And even though a man may not want to have children, leaving him open to date women his age or older, how many men are attracted to women who look as old as they are? Or, God forbid, older? Especially you men over forty. Those of you who don't care what a woman looks like, who are able to appreciate a woman for her personality or intelligence alone, fall into the category I call *"the exceptional few"* which I discuss in the next chapter.

The data I researched explained so much to me that I finally realized men could no more change their hardwiring than women could. I stopped blaming them for their tendency to be visual, and started teaching women how to look youthful and feminine, be more approachable, and stop alienating men by criticizing them for their natural tendencies. I am not always happy that men are the way they are, but now I understand why. I know I can't hope to change years of social conditioning, let alone biological destiny in my lifetime.

The more things change, the more the basics remain the same. The female desire to be courted, cared for and protected remains a constant in the complex maneuverings of a world where generation xers tattoo their skin, pierce their tongues and breed in the glow of the internet. Romance isn't dead, it's just needs a nooner. Women continue to want from men what they've always wanted. Our ancestors must have done something right or we wouldn't be here to fight about how they did it all wrong.

Ask yourself, do you want to get some women in your life, or do you want to sit around complaining about how crazy women are while other guys are out with them, *doing what you'd like to be doing*? You are not going to change years of conditioning by society, her parents, or mother nature by being right. You can be right and alone, or you can *do* something about your odds. So let's get on with it. It's time someone told you what women really want and it's time for women to give you what you deserve.

I hope you enjoy the book and I hope that you use it.

Jama Clark, Ph.D.
San Francisco, California 1997

"You are totally unique – just like everybody else."

—*Anon*

The 1 Exceptional Few

Everyone hates stereotypes. The word stereotype is used as a negative label for frequently occurring behavior; however, not all stereotypes are negative. For example, most men enjoy sports and most women like to shop. These stereotypic behaviors are well-known and accepted habits of both sexes. When it comes to mating, there are also patterns of behavior-preferences shall we say, that occur frequently as well.

When I began teaching men and women which personal characteristics the opposite sex was attracted to, one or two people in each of my seminars always took exception. They didn't like being lumped into a category that they didn't agree with. I don't blame them. As a result, I spent a lot of time saying, "Well, there is always the man who really *likes* short hair on women, or the thirty-five-year-old guy who finds fifty year-old women attractive, or the man who *doesn't* notice or care that a woman has huge thighs." Later, I began labeling these people with infrequently occurring preferences *"the exceptional few."*

I use the term in my seminars to avoid lengthy "exception to the rule" speeches. I use it in this book to refer to women who like male behavior that falls outside the norm. The word <u>norm</u> represents <u>commonly occurring</u> preferences among women, for example, most women prefer men without mustaches. The phrase *exceptional few* means a small, select group of women and represents a less frequent opinion.

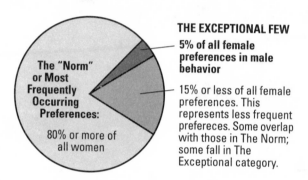

THE EXCEPTIONAL FEW

The "Norm" or Most Frequently Occurring Preferences:

80% or more of all women

5% of all female preferences in male behavior

15% or less of all female preferences. This represents less frequent prefereces. Some overlap with those in The Norm; some fall in The Exceptional category.

So, falling into the <u>exceptional</u> five percent would be:

- A woman who has sex with a man without attaching a lot of meaning to it.
- A woman who doesn't care about what a man does for a living or how much money he makes.
- A woman who accepts a man who is poor or struggling financially as marriage material.
- A woman who is initially attracted to a man that is much shorter than she is.

I'm sorry! I know these realities may hurt; but yes, women who fall into "the norm" have standards similar to these.

Throughout this book I use the term <u>exceptionally few</u> instead of saying you-might-find-a-woman-who-will-accept-you-despite-the-fact-that-you. . . have a gold ring through your nostril, drink excessively, live at home with your parents at age thirty, dress like a nomadic monk, are shorter than she is, don't bathe regularly or behave passively. If you have other behaviors that women in the norm don't find attractive, (see *Chapter Four, Why You Are Not Attracting Women and What To Do About It*), exceptionally few women will be attracted to them.

In the coming chapters, I outline the most common behaviors that attract women and teach you how to acquire and master these traits. It is extremely important to learn what *most* women respond to in order to increase your success rate. Learning and adapting to what works with the majority of women will get you farther and faster than hunting for that rare, unique woman who is not part of the pack.

Why shouldn't you hunt for a woman who can accept your weaknesses and idiosyncrasies? *You should!* And you'd be a lot happier if you found one of these rare gems. But, quite frankly, most people are lazy and don't want to put in the time and energy to work that hard. Let's face it, if you can't even get yourself out of the house to meet women regularly, you will certainly not be able to find a needle in a haystack. Both sexes tend to choose the best mate they can find after spending very little effort, time, or energy searching. That's because most people discourage easily. They don't consider how they may be contributing to the problem and blame outside circumstances for their failures. Maybe if we spent more time looking for and screening our mates, the divorce rate wouldn't be at fifty percent and you wouldn't have to spend so much money on self-help books!

Imagine that you are looking for a new car and only go to three car lots. You will settle on the best deal that you can negotiate after you have checked out the cars in all three lots. Now imagine that you talked with one hundred car dealerships all over your state and compared the cost of each city's tax, shipping, as well as the price mark-ups of each dealer. You haggle, hang in there and outfox the sales-people. You contact wholesalers and cruise the net for the best deals. Of course you'll get a better deal with better options than you would by searching through only three lots!

People who put more effort into their relationships might get counseling, change cities or jobs, upgrade their clothing, lose weight, style their hair differently, shave their mustaches, stop smoking or even consider plastic surgery. They take classes such as the ones I offer on body language or conversational skills, and often go out at least two times a week to different places to find dates. They make finding a girl the first priority in their lives instead of second or third behind their hobbies, the TV or their computer. When you put that much energy into something, you get results.

Given the availability of mates, and the resources we use, we end up with the best person we can attract from whatever size pool we fish in, large or small. If you want to catch a big fish, you have to swim with the sharks. If you want to go to the show, you have learn to hit like the pros. You have to want it and want it bad!

If you improve your resources, job status, physical appearance, mental attitude and use more search strategies you will have a larger pool of women to pick from. In addition, going out to larger events will increase your odds tremendously. I call this the "shotgun" approach; it covers the most territory and attracts the most women in the least amount of time. Think quantity as well as quality. What? Oh. You don't *like* singles events or large groups of people? Well then, you'll just have fewer cars to choose from because you only took the time to look through a few lots.

In a larger group you are more likely to find a woman who will be willing to accept your weaknesses along with your strengths. According to my observation and studies from other professionals in the field, exceptionally few women will want to accept your weaknesses along with your better qualities if you have one or more "low cards." Your less than desirable traits are liabilities that you must address in order to attract the majority of women. (Again, See Chapter Four, *Why You Are Not Attracting Women and What To Do About It*, where I list these low cards.)

There are a few exceptions to this rule. For example, women who have been alone for long periods of time usually tend to be more open-minded about accepting a broader range of qualities. Eccentric women, some artistic types, masculine women, or women who had fathers with traits similar to yours may be more tolerant. Older women, for example, are certainly more accepting and understanding. Did you know that for every available single man over the age of sixty, there are seven available single women? This is not only due to the fact that men are under more stress and die earlier, but because women marry older men and their husbands die before they do! So, if you aren't having luck now, just wait until you're an old codger-things will be peachy!

When women are scarce, things get even harder. Alaskan men, for example, tend to be much more forgiving toward women who carry weight or who are older than they are because there are fewer women to go around. One man who lives way out in the Aleutian chain told me that men hang on to their girlfriends like glue in public because they don't want someone to snatch them away. The girls up there have a saying:

"The odds are good, but the goods are odd."

Female promiscuity is higher where women are scarce, so the men have a saying too:

"You don't lose your girlfriend, you just lose your turn."

Needless to say, Alaska is a place where it is difficult to score. Easy sex (if that is an accurate term) and better dating odds are more readily found in warmer climates where women have more competition. In more populated areas, women with lower self-esteem are more likely to be persuaded that if they don't date you, you'll find someone else.

Clearly, you can stay exactly the way you are and find a girl. You don't *have* to learn new behaviors that will attract the most women. You don't *have* to change your attitude, stop belching or bring roses to anyone! But, will you want the kind of woman who is attracted to you the way you are, flaws and all? Perhaps more importantly, why will she want you?

Let me give you an example. One of the women in my women's class was about twenty pounds overweight. I asked her if she was willing to go out with a man who was also overweight, what would seem to be her match given her present physical status, (for a man in the norm doesn't find overweight women attractive.) She said no! *She* was attracted to good-looking, thin men. What a double standard! She got the message and is losing weight rapidly. She wasn't willing to drop her standards and she *was* willing to change in order to attract the kind of man she wanted. Would you do the same?

Here's another example: A male client who continually strikes out with women can't understand why he isn't dating; he says he tries hard to meet women, and he has a job that pays well. He's attracted to "8's, 9's and 10's," but he has average looks and is balding at a somewhat early age. In order for him to attract women who are considerably better looking than he is, he will have to 1) have a high-paying job, and 2) have a great personality. Well, he has a great job, but he also has a defeatist attitude, as well as the "nice guy-doormat" syndrome, which I explain in the next chapter. His negative attitude was turning women off. This man refuses to look at women who are of the same level of attractiveness that he is, but he resists the fact that he has a negative attitude. *"Exceptionally few"* "8, 9, or 10" females will find him attractive.

The last client I talked to hadn't dated in fifteen years, and after a speech about how difficult women were, asked me what he was doing wrong. I told him it might be hard for him to hear, did he want to hear it? Yes, yes, he did. I then suggested that if he lost his pot belly and polished up his nervous humor, he would do better. He protested loudly. I found out later that he was a serious alcoholic. We are all human; most of us would rather stumble along not facing our issues and wait until we get really lonely or sick before we do something about our problems. He disappeared and two years passed; I saw him again and suggested that he lose weight and watch his drinking. He was having trouble with his blood pressure, and other physical reactions to the booze, and of course, he was dateless. I hope he will make it out of his loneliness, but I doubt it. Are you listening, Jim?

Remember, a woman's preference in men is instinctual, bio-logical, and largely unconscious. It is reinforced through her socialization and upbringing, as well as the media. She will have a difficult time finding your eccentric behavior attractive, unless she is unusual and has managed to resist the social influences around her.

It's the *exceptional* woman who can love a shorter guy with a pot belly and large love handles or the man in financial difficulty; It's the more evolved, aware female who can see your deeper qualities, who will accept your shortcomings and not try to fix you. It is this type of woman who will appreciate you for who you <u>are</u>, not who you <u>will be</u>. This woman is an individualist who does not run with the pack. And yes, the older she is, the more depth she usually has. She is more likely to be accepting of your flaws because she has lived longer, and had to overcome some adversity. This kind of female has learned that wealth and good looks are not everything. She can see through jerky behavior and she looks for real quality in a man.

TRAITS OF THE EXCEPTIONAL WOMAN
WHO HAS PROBLEMS

Not all "exceptional" behavior is exceptionally healthy. Here is a partial list of traits that women who don't fall into the norm may have:

- She is more likely to be independent and outspoken.

- She may have a strong temper and think nothing of using it.

- She may accept you just the way you are; but be extremely quiet and withdrawn; this quietness could mask sexual abuse or extremely disturbed behavior.

- She is more likely to dislike traditional "female" behaviors, such as cooking, cleaning, general caretaking, child bearing and/or feminine dressing.

- She may not plan to marry and might insist on counseling.

- She might have a lot of money and not mind supporting you!

- If you are an alcoholic, she might accept that but withdraw sexually or she might have an addiction to add to yours! You two would make a great team.

- If you're overly accommodating, she might tolerate it because her particular quirk will not be confronted by you—like her affairs or her lack of sex drive.

But, with luck and a lot of hunting you might find a true gem. The "exceptional" woman without problems is often extremely aware and evolved. She has a spiritual sense of herself, is grounded and will not care much what you look like, how much money you make or how tall you are. But guys - this kind of woman usually has some lines on her face and...SHE MAY EVEN BE OVERWEIGHT! (You knew there had to be a catch!)

Listen closely. Would you want the kind of woman who is more likely to accept you just the way you are? And are you willing to love and tolerate <u>her</u> weaknesses in exchange for accepting you? In short, <u>are you willing to give up the more physically attractive woman</u>? Unfortunately, because as a male you mate visually, you probably don't want to do this. From a woman's point of view, many of you are stubborn enough to believe that *you* are different, *you* are unique, *you* have no problems! You can have it all and shouldn't have to change. (It's just a matter of luck and fate, you think.) I wish I could agree with you. And so, most of you will go home alone and get older searching in vain for that perfect princess without figuring out your own issues.

Do not try to teach a pig to sing.
It is a waste of time, and it annoys the pig.

Well, let's look at your cards. What *do* you have to entice the younger, more beautiful, higher-status female? Are you wealthy or at least considerably more well-off than she is? Do you drive a nice car? Do you own your own home? Can you afford to take her out to nice places? Are you tall? At least three inches taller than she is? Are you well-educated? Can you talk about your weaknesses, and have you addressed your emotional development? Have you had some counseling? (A positive point!) Do you stand up for yourself and your opinions? The higher-status female will be looking for all of these qualities in a man.

A beautiful, younger, intelligent, friendly, slender woman can have just about any man she chooses (until she ages of course.) If she can attract a man who is handsome, tall, and financially successful, why not? Is it any surprise that those of you who are not what society and the Marlboro Man taught us "a man" ought to be are striking out with these women? In order to attract a high-status women,(and by that I mean the higher the status of the woman, the more desirable she is,) you have to have some *bargaining tools*, which I will discuss in the coming chapters.

I tell the members of my men's classes that they can all have a "10," <u>but will they want the personality that often comes with her</u>? Like the handsome male, the beautiful female has had opportunities come her way because of her looks. Usually, she has not had to work for much; she has often been taken care of financially, either by her father or by the men in her life. She may have been divorced several times. She might have children; if so, she certainly wants a man who can help out financially. Or, she may be an aging beauty who has finally discovered all that glitters is not gold.

A female "10" (beauty, a good body, a youthful appearance, a good personality) who <u>would</u> choose a man who is not a "10" (looks, financial stability, height and emotional depth) usually falls into one of three categories:

1. **She will mate with a man with average looks because he has wealth, power, or high self-esteem.** (Note that high self-esteem for men is often linked with money.) She "trades" getting a better looking man for these balancing traits.

2. **She will choose a man with extremely good looks, but a poor income.** She "trades" financial security for the narcissistic charm of this man who may often be younger than she is. In this case, she may have more money than he does. In Hollywood, they label these men "boy toys."

3. **She has some hidden personality problems.** He is able to attract her by accepting her less than desirable personality traits. *The question is, do you want high maintenance?*

So, if she's a "10" all around, she can get a "10" in all categories, too. If you don't rank at the top, or even at a nine or an eight in the attributes that attract women, (like ninety percent of the rest of the guys), you have a decision. You can cling to your wish list and be alone, or you can learn to appreciate a woman who matches you in status and attractiveness. You can choose to "date where you can date." To be blunt-you can lower your standards. . . . Are you still there?

If you are not willing to do this, you can boost your bargaining ability, which this book teaches. This is the toughest route, and it requires hard work. You thought this was going to be easy, huh? No, not easy, but realistic. Easy sells books. Real takes work. And if you don't want to accept that, I've got this great five dollar watch I'd like to sell you.

When I was looking for a publisher for this book a few years back, one editor said, "I don't think men want to be told that women are not attracted to short, overweight, balding men with low paychecks. They want to be told that they can get any women they want" . . .

> . . . just like women want to be told
> that being fat doesn't matter.

I decided not to sell dreams; I decided to teach the truth, adaptation and how men can make the most out of what they have. And nothing is completely impossible. I use Mickey Rooney as an example. He's short, pudgy, balding and has attracted women all his life. What does he have? A positive outlook, charisma, talent, and money. Now, some of <u>those</u> traits can be learned or acquired. About the only thing you can't do much about is height, and even that can be impressively enhanced through clothing, color choice, and a powerful attitude (see Chapter Nine for further details.)

If you can't figure out why you aren't attracting women, get some consultation, some <u>objective</u> feedback from someone other than your roommate or your mother and **do something** about what is getting in your way. We cannot see ourselves as others see us! Until you learn or earn more bargaining tools you will be frustrated in your search for a beautiful woman who will accept you the way you are, or, far more likely . . .

You will attract women of the same level of attractiveness and power that you are.
A universal law

Remember, "As ye sow, so shall ye reap." Here is another enlightening way I heard this put:

"If you suck, so do your relationships."

Moving right along, it all comes down to self-esteem. If you feel lousy about yourself, you will attract women who will treat you the same way. Your lack of self-esteem will show itself through the various struggles in the relationships that you have. If women don't leave you, *they will stay with you and treat you as badly as you are treating yourself.* You are not going to find the perfect princess who will rescue you from your self-destructive habits. Instead, these habits will be reinforced by each woman, or made worse. Take care of your problems or they will take care of you.

Some women are now getting the message that finding and fixing men is not the answer to their unhappiness. When I give my lectures on dating to both sexes, one of the first things I say is that my class is not about what is wrong with the opposite sex. First, you have to deal with what's happening on *your* side of the fence, not criticize your neighbor's gardening. Plus, it's a hell of a lot easier to weed your own yard than to reach over the fence and weed somebody else's.

The fact that the majority of people in counseling are female indicates that women are more willing to confront their issues, *not* that they are worse off psychologically than men. We all grew up with the <u>same</u> kinds of parents, some supportive, some not so supportive. We all went to about the <u>same</u> kinds of schools and had mostly the same kinds of experiences. Did *all* of the women receive worse parenting than men did, thus causing a mass migration into counseling? **Or do you think that women got a worse deal than *men* did due to our "patriarchal society"?** I think not! In fact, most women will tell you that they would never trade places with a man, given the way that men were raised to suppress their feelings.

I continually ask the younger men I work with if it was OK for them to cry on the playground when they were little and they continue to say no. Men grow up controlling their emotions, working hard, and becoming enraged that women don't appreciate them. <u>What profit a man to gain the world and lose his soul?</u>

Perhaps it is due to the AIDS crisis, but I strongly suspect that one of the primary reasons more men are now seeking counseling is that *women are not having sex as often as they used to.* If you haven't been dating for a long time, consider getting some help.

No matter why men are now considering counseling, I am glad to be a part of it. We are all in this boat together. If you are truly sick of being alone, you need to learn what attracts the largest number of women or you need to hunt fiercely for the "exceptional few." Let's start looking at what may be getting in your way.

**And let's begin with what
women <u>really</u> want.**

"I know not
which lives more
unnatural lives—
obeying husbands
or commanding wives."

—*Benjamin Franklin*

Doormat 2 or Jerk?

would like to share with you a system that will help
clear up some of the problems you may be having with
women. "Jerk" and "Doormat" are unpleasant words—
nobody likes to be classified, and neither should you.
The psychological profession, for example, conveniently
lumps people into categories based on their behaviors. The
clinical term for a man with "jerk" characteristics might be
narcissistic or even *sociopathic,* and a man who lets women
push him around might be called *passive-aggressive.* Psychological diagnosis is not an exact science. However, our profession does this for the same reason that basketball fans
call a "fastbreak" a quick run away from the opponent down
to the opposite side of the court. Using fastbreak is quicker,
and most fans know what it means without using all those
words. Most men definitely know the meaning of "jerk,"
and even some jerks know who they are. "Sure I'm a jerk,"
he said to me, "But I'm a *nice* jerk." Typical.

In this chapter, I discuss men who have the tendency to be
either like a "jerk" or a "doormat." I use these terms to avoid
having to constantly say, "Well, there is always the guy who
puts up a cool outer image, has difficulty getting close and
often mistreats women. I use these terms not to trivialize
your situation, but to offer a concrete reminder so you can
avoid the type of behavior that women find unattractive. I
strongly suggest that you read further into the psychology

of personality development if you really want to understand the finer points of why you behave the way you do around women. I have included under each category several possible reasons why you may have acquired these kinds of behaviors.

Look at the scale below.

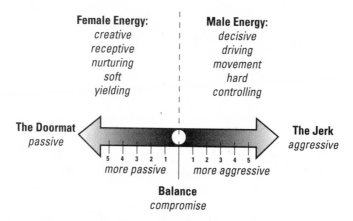

Female Energy:
creative
receptive
nurturing
soft
yielding

Male Energy:
decisive
driving
movement
hard
controlling

The Doormat
passive

The Jerk
aggressive

5 4 3 2 1   1 2 3 4 5
more passive | *more aggressive*

Balance
compromise

This graph represents a number line with "jerk" behavior at one end, and "doormat" behavior at the one hundred eighty degree opposite. The zero point represents a balance between these two extremes. Let's talk about the "doormat" and the "jerk" set of male behaviors and how women react to them.

THE JERK

"Jerk" is a term that both men and women seem to understand. The jerk is the guy you always see with women. He is usually charming and is often good-looking or wealthy. He's the guy who gets away with mistreating people; he takes care of himself first, and usually at the expense of others. He's a superb salesman who knows how to charm and manipulate. Women think he's incredibly sexy and he usually knows how to get them into bed—those who aren't wise to him don't call him a jerk until *after* he's broken their hearts. Before he leaves her (or gets her to leave him), he's considered to be mysterious, exciting and unpredictable. He wines her, dines her, and then disappears, returning just in time to woo her back, using the off again on again influence technique of <u>intermittent reinforcement</u> that is discussed in Chapter Eleven. Men who aren't jerks watch his tactics with disbelief and hidden admiration and my male clients and friends say they can't *believe* that women stupidly fall for the lines and lies that the jerk gives them, basically to get laid. Unfortunately, the tactics of the jerk often work with gullible women.

THE DOORMAT

At the opposite end of the scale is "the doormat," who accepts being treated just like one. He lets women wipe their feet on him. He practically lies down and says "walk on me." He is usually quiet and unassuming, but always VERY HELPFUL. He's a good Boy Scout! He's trusty and does his duty to be there when we need him! Like, at two a.m. after a jerk has dumped us, he'd be willing to get out of bed and pick us up from the telephone booth we've fled to. He's a shoulder to cry on. He's *great* at moving our furniture. . . loaning money. . . good for ever-so-many dinners out. **He is definitely not sexy!** A clinical description for this type of man is *co-dependent*. He hopes in vain that, if he just loves us enough, **if he just tries hard enough,** we will see him for the knight in shining armor who he is, and give up on all the jerks. Wrong!

Letting a woman treat you like a doormat sounds really lame, doesn't it? But ninety-nine percent of all the men I see in my classes or individually as clients exhibit these passive behaviors. In my seminars I say: Most of you in this room are probably nice guys; why should any jerks come to my seminars?. . . *They have women hanging all over them.* **Why should *they* possibly think they need help?** Of course the "jerks" *do* need help, for healthy women will eventually leave to choose a more balanced, giving man.

<u>There is nothing wrong with being a "nice guy" and treating women well.</u> That's not the point here. In fact, women

are attracted to you *because* you treat them decently. It is your most endearing quality. After a first date we say *"he's so nice"* and we mean it. But, after the second or third date, if there isn't some additional spice, this niceness begins to wear thin and gets more and more boring. We are attracted to your sweet, nurturing behavior—but we won't stay with you just because of it! We will merely leave you if there isn't more to you than your niceness. ***Even worse, we could marry you and make your life miserable!***

A doormat has *lots* of niceness (remember, it's a matter of degree), a long-suffering attitude, and a feeling of helplessness to do anything about it. He feels trapped under this behavior and doesn't know how to get out. Underneath, he's often angry at being taken for granted. That's where the label aggressive, in "passive-aggressive" comes in. On the surface, he appears to go along with her pushiness; underneath, he's fuming. He has usually conditioned her to treat him like this by not speaking up; and/or he doesn't have the skills to be able to stop the situation.

Some Female Views on Niceness:

1. You always agree with what we say—***boring!***

2. You rarely express opinions that aren't ours or someone else's—***ditto.***

3. You don't initiate ideas or adventures other than what we suggest (even <u>we</u> find ourselves tiresome and need other stimulation.)

4. You don't talk very much—**anybody home?**

5. And finally—

   WHY SHOULD WE GET IN BED WITH YOU WHEN YOU ARE SO PREDICTABLE OUT OF IT?

Sexual expression is one of surrendering to another. But we can't surrender to you because you've already given in to us! "You aren't a challenge." In animal language, not being a challenge means you are the weaker one of the pair, and as females, *we want to choose the strongest.* If we can control you by criticizing you, pushing you around, having you at our beck and call, we can't find you attractive. But, as harsh as this sounds, there is an unconscious reasoning to this:

If the man can't stand up to us, what's going to happen when some *real* danger threatens?

And so, we tend to choose in the direction of the jerk, whose outward behavior suggests that he is in charge. Speaking for the majority of the women out there, both as a professional and as a woman who has fallen for her share of jerks, let me tell you why these bad boys appeal to us. To be succinct:

> *The "jerks" of the world let us know that they*
> *cannot possibly be controlled, and women love*
> *men they can't possibly hope to control.*

Does this mean that I'm advocating being a jerk? No way! So what's the answer? Don't give up your kindness and your gentleness—these are your strengths! Just add to them. Offer us both the excitement and unpredictability that the jerk seems to have <u>and</u> the warmth and caring of the doormat. Give us both. This requires taking care of yourself and NOT LETTING YOURSELF BE MISTREATED.

On the number line between jerkdom and doormatdom is the balance area, ideally around zero. A man who has balance does not allow himself to be mistreated like a doormat, and he doesn't act abusive or distant like the jerk when a real opportunity for love shows up. Where do you think you are this line? Do you err on the side of being taken advantage of? Or are you more of a jerk? A good way to figure this out is to consider the number of times you have instigated break-ups versus how often the woman has broken up with you. First, take a moment to figure this out. What is your tendency?

(Thinking music floats down from the speakers.)

Now, with this pattern in your mind—and this is very important—try to remember *the reasons* she gave for leaving you.

What Is She Saying?

- She "really wants to be your friend."
- She "doesn't feel romantically about you."
- You "are really important to her" —*as a friend.*
- She doesn't know why but she says "it doesn't feel right."
- She is "not ready for a relationship right now."
- You are "not her type."
- *She's sorry, "but she just can't seem to get over Ricardo!"*

If the above phrases sound familiar, and have been repeated by more than one woman as she dumped you, you are being overly nice and are headed for DOORMAT CITY... YOU'VE JUST BEEN LJBF'd ! (Let's Just Be Friends'd) Be direct! Ask what her intentions are. Is she interested in you or not? Stop wasting your time trying to decipher sign language. She will often come right out with it. If she is just plain vague in general, and you can't get a definite statement about how she feels about you (because, let's face it, you are probably spending a lot of money on her and doing LOTS of things for her that she doesn't want to give up) then consider her *behavior.*

What Is She Doing?

- Breaking dates?
- Saying she will and then she won't?
- Talking about her other relationships in front of you or constantly bringing up her ex?
- Avoiding sex or engaging in occasional but not so passionate kisses? (Note: She may even sleep with you, but it is extremely sporadic.)
- Dating other men while you wait patiently for her to come to her senses?
- Always busy with work, just doesn't have time this week or next and waffles when you try to pin her down to a definite date? (But wants you to come over and fix her CD player?)

- Warming up to you when you spend money on her and fix the CD player but pulling away from you when you try to kiss her after several dates? (Note: Make sure you have dated her a reasonable amount of time before assuming she's not interested because she doesn't want to get physical.)
- Giving you kisses, but doesn't seem to have her heart in it? (Do you *enjoy* those dry little chicken pecks?)

These behaviors are giveaways that you are being taken for granted. **You must quit it immediately if you want to have a relationship with her and enjoy any sex!**

If, on the other hand, women are leaving you after a lot of fire and fury, your girlfriend tells you she wants you to **talk to her**, that she is sick of your working, skiing, traveling, womanizing, and generally **not paying enough attention to her** or giving her what she needs *emotionally*— you probably have the problem of being more of a jerk. You can't let women get close to you and you are afraid of intimacy. You have difficulty talking about your feelings and your vulnerabilities. OK, so we *are* attracted to your forceful attitude, your charm, and your money. But that doesn't make up for your waffling behavior and your distancing. When you *do* start to open up, and we start coming toward you, you back away. A smart woman eventually wises up to this yo-yo behavior and will find a man who is ready to go deeper.

WHY YOU STARTED ACTING THIS WAY

The Jerk

There of course are no "jerks" any more than there are "gold-diggers," only men who were trained and chose to act that way since early childhood because it was safer.

This man wasn't loved or given praise for who <u>he</u> was as a young boy—but he was given attention for his performance and appearance. And so being the best, beating others and the constant conquest for getting attention continues to be a theme as he ages. The youngest woman, the fastest car, the best stockbroker, the latest version. Average doesn't cut it. Covering up his real feelings, especially feelings of failure becomes the name of his game. When I met my last jerk, he informed me within the first half hour of meeting me that he had been unfaithful to his wife, that he had dated "a runner-up for Miss Universe" and that he had put away close to a million for his childrens' college education. The fact that he hadn't stopped drinking in twenty years was conveniently left out. . . .

When this man did show his feelings, or failed, he was humiliated and put down by his family's code of "what a man should be." He discovered that in order to be loved he had to be perfect, to hide his vulnerabilities. Acting tough usually worked. Praise came only when he was a star. One friend's wife reported that her brother, a star athlete, missed going to the Olympics by mere seconds. His father, who attended the track meet said only, "You should have run faster." Who can always be first? This man finds it much easier not to care these days and gets himself into tight situations trying to avoid defeat. He walls himself off by learning not to lean on anyone; the closer a woman comes to him, the more threatened he gets. If he gets too close, then she'll find out that he's fallible just like everyone else. Behind this protective wall he feels empty, doesn't know who he is; he just knows how to run his cover-up act and fills up his emptiness with a parade of women, high-powered business activities, and risky behavior. Ready sex fills the emptiness—so do alcohol, drugs and expensive toys.

He tends to choose very good looking women who cater to him and give him the adoration he requires. He basks in the reflected glory of his newest conquest. The outer appearance is extremely important to him— how he looks, how she looks, and how others view him. He's intolerant of any flaws. She's got large thighs? Next!

Even very patient women may not be able to get through the armor that this man protects himself with. He lives much of his emotional life alone until he gets help, if ever. When these lonely men finally have been lonely long enough, their wives leave them because of their affairs or their drinking, their work goes badly, or their internal stress mounts to the point that they are extremely dissatisfied with their lives (they often can't put their finger on what it is, they just feel lousy)—they sometimes get help. But this is usually *after* they are in crisis.

Most of the time, the jerk eventually chooses a woman who worships him and doesn't confront his distant behavior. This type of woman will accept what crumbs of intimacy she can get, just being happy to bask in the glow of his power and the objects he gives her. She feels protected by his money or position. The jerk often has affairs, women in every port, and will rarely divorce his wife unless he is seriously in love enough to risk court costs and child support. It is the long-suffering, dutiful wife who props this lonely guy up and gives him some sense of stability. This is why his mistress will rarely be able to pry him from home. His wife is a rock, but an anchor to which he can never fully commit, or he would realize his huge need and feel overwhelmed. The wife is certainly not a challenge for him, so in order to avoid feeling how empty he is, he has affairs. When his mistress demands his full attention, threatening a crack in his emotional armor, the wife looks appealing again. With her, he never has to change and always finds allegiance. **"Better the devil we know than the devil we don't know."**

If he doesn't have affairs he will control his wife's spending and her activities, keeping her emotionally captive (through her co-dependency) so that he will have her to save him from the feelings of inadequacy that always threaten to surface. When his demands become excessive, sometimes she gets out, but rarely before she is verbally and sometimes physically abused. She knows he needs her and to an insecure woman this is very important.

It is much harder for the "jerk" to change than it is for the doormat. The jerk usually continues to attract women, so he never feels alone. The kindly doormat stands a much better chance of changing. He at least is able to feel that something is wrong because he isn't dating regularly and women often leave him.

The Doormat

To get love, this man became a people pleaser. He believes that who he is isn't good enough, that he has to earn his love. Consider this list of contributing factors and see whether any of the situations sound familiar to you.

1. An early illness leaves him dependent upon caretaking. His mother becomes vigilant and he grows up learning that a strong female caretaker or Mom is necessary to his survival. He defers to women and he chooses strong, take charge types.

2. A younger sibling is born within two years of his birth. Just about the time his personality is forming, Mom has to spend more time with the new baby. He learns to defer his own needs to his younger sibling and takes in the idea that he is not important enough. He learns that if he wants love, he has to wait.

3. He has a verbally overbearing mother or father. He can't fight this, so to stay out of this parent's way he learns to be quiet and disappear into the woodwork, which is very smart move.

4. One of his parents abused drugs, the environment felt dangerous, and his best protection was to withdraw.

5. His parents were both low-keyed individuals and he patterned himself after them.

6. His mother died when he was young, or his mother or father were noticeably absent and he had to fend for himself.

7. His parents were extremely religious, and he feels guilty when he doesn't act like a good boy. He is taught that sex is bad. He is rewarded when he acts reserved and contained. Expressions of emotions are frowned upon.

8. He lived in a home that was remote or isolated from other kids and he didn't learn to socialize.

9. He was a firstborn and was unable to meet up to his parents' expectations. Firstborns usually have more pressure put on them.

10. His parents were in the military or other work that caused his family to move. He was not able to make a strong connection with others, and so he learned to go inside himself, to become quiet, and to comfort himself.

11. He was not as good-looking or athletic as his other siblings and grew up feeling like an ugly duckling.

12. He was overweight, very small, or very tall when he grew up. He felt out of place or different and withdrew to avoid calling attention to himself

13. His academic skills were slow to mature. He was put in a "special" class, or held back and thought there was "something wrong" with him. This feeling may follow him throughout life.

14. He was brighter than most of the other kids and felt different because the teacher made an example of him. His shyness was due to other kids teasing or shutting him out.

15. He was adopted late or spent time moving from one family to another due to divorce or family problems. He learned to deal with this by going inward and licking his own wounds.

Massive social unrest and loneliness lead all of us to regard the outside world as dangerous, and we withdraw into our own world. We live far more isolated lives than ever before in this century. The violence that is happening all around us, the high divorce rate together with the constant moving that most families do contribute to our isolation. Turning inward is an instinctual response if we have grown up without close family ties.

As you can see, there are many reasons why you withdrew and learned to be quiet. Psychologists also believe that people are actually born with a tendency toward a certain type of disposition, shy or outgoing. Our socialization then either reinforces or re-forms these genetic traits into the behaviors we now rely on as adults.

There is a third possibility as well, that you may be doing both types of behavior with different women. Look back at the patterns of your last relationships. Did you act like a doormat around one woman (or several)—you worshipped and adored her and let her run you around? Chances are she broke up with you. Then, did you try to avoid "that" kind of woman by choosing a girl who was the diametrically opposed opposite? For example, was your first wife a raving witch, and was your second wife a pushover? Maybe you are "overcorrecting."

If so, you are still faced with some kind of "stuck " behavior that probably came from your parents. Were they different as night and day? Did Dad boss you around, and did you identify with your long-suffering mom? Or was Mom the loudmouth and did you grow up to be like your meek and mild Pop? If you are more like the jerk, you can see this pattern in your parents too. The jerk takes on the qualities of the dominant parent, the parent who usually got their way. Either role—the submissive doormat or the overbearing jerk—are behaviors that you used to compensate for your inability to treat yourself with respect.

Whichever pattern you wound up with, you don't have to hang onto it forever. It's true that people rarely change their nature, but with enough desire (or pain), you can learn more balance. Or, you can sit it out and imagine that if you just found the right woman, everything would work out. This is kind of like hoping that somehow you will win the lottery. At least half of the male population once thought they had the right woman too—until a divorce changed their minds.

As the years passed, quiet, outwardly tolerant behavior (with occasional outbursts of well-deserved anger!) took many shy men through hard times. But unassuming behavior didn't work well with the girls in high school, and unfortunately, it continues to be unattractive to older women as well. *What worked for you as a child cannot work for you as a fully functioning adult.* You must learn some balance and get out of your own world if you want to relate to others on a regular basis. Figure out what your patterns are so you can learn to control them, and they don't control you. Doormat or jerk, either way, you're a lonely camper, bucko.

You might be interested to know that, when a woman is asked to choose between jerk qualities or doormat qualities on the doormat-jerk scale, privately, among women, if she had to choose one set of behaviors she will chose the jerk qualities. I have taught relationship classes for women now for more than ten years and in every class I survey, the more assertive traits are what women want. I hear this over and over from men. "Women say they want sensitive men, but they really don't." And you are partially right. Women *want* to appreciate the nice guy, but they just can't get themselves to do it. And there is a perfectly logical explanation for this strange behavior. It is extremely important that you understand why women want more independent behavior, or you'll be forever blaming them for it, *and you'll also be alone a lot longer.*

Before I explain why women can't get themselves to appreciate the nice guy, let me say that this situation is not your fault. And sorry, but it isn't the woman's fault either. As men, you were not encouraged to talk things out or express your feelings. Was it *cool* to cry on the playground if you were a boy? Right. Instead, you acted like you didn't care, you could take it. And so, as you aged you either toughened up or withdrew. Men in most societies are taught that power means acting tough and independent, and physical force is the way to show that power. But society is changing far too fast for years of conditioning to catch up with these changes. Men are learning quickly that they can no longer use their bodies to dominate women. Some are facing harassment cases or even criminal charges. So, what other course can a man take when he is threatened? Some men choose passivity, and some men explode or revert to hitting. But others are now learning a far better and primarily safer power source: **words**.

The human female, who is usually smaller and can still be overpowered physically by the male, had to learn to live by her wits, to depend upon <u>her words</u> to get her out of dangerous situations. So, she fights verbally, and the male, not allowed to fight with his body anymore due to societal constraints, often withdraws.

No wonder you get confused, angry, or refuse to cooperate when a woman asks you to open up and talk. It feels like a double message! By showing your soft side, you are going against everything society has taught you "a man" ought to be! When a woman asks you to talk, she is asking you to fight with her *on her terms*. And to make matters even more complicated, the man who talks *too* much sometimes appears overly feminine. Of course he does, for it is a <u>female strength</u>! Remember the phrase "strong and silent"?

This is the reason women say they want a sensitive man, but have trouble accepting him. When you *do* talk to us and let us know that you love us, we don't know how to handle it. We *too* have been conditioned to see aloof and unfeeling men as "strong." Many of our fathers were strong and silent as well. If our image of love is one of restraint, when we see real love coming we sometimes get confused. This is often why gentle, soft-spoken men do not do well with women. Women are suffering from the same social stereotypes that men are. We desperately need to learn how to accept loving men into our lives, just as men need to learn to express their feelings verbally.

You've lived through many years of your parents and society telling you how a man ought to be, and what you have learned isn't working the way you want it to. You either are not getting the women you want to stay in your life, or worse, aren't attracting women to begin with. If you are a quiet man, you learned early on that it wasn't safe to talk back to

Mom or Dad. You learned your best defense was being quiet and passive, or acting like you didn't care. If you spoke up, you were scolded or put down. <u>It was a smart strategy</u>. Perhaps you also were picked on at school because of your height, weight, intelligence, or other traits which set you apart from the others. Some of you experienced divorce, constantly moved or had what I call a "life trauma,"— a tragic physical or emotional event that delayed your development as a man. All of these circumstances helped form your current communication patterns with women.

Some men are now embarking on a healing process, learning to open their hearts to women. The men's movement is now empowering men to <u>set their limits with women</u> and to get in touch with their *inner* strengths.

Remember, this book isn't about how to change society, it's about **what to do <u>now</u> to attract women.** Most of you continue to use behaviors that you learned long ago. In the past, those behaviors worked to protect you from situations over which you had little choice or control. But this is the present, and you *do* have control over what will happen to you both now and in the future. You *can* change the way you act. You *can* attract women who will appreciate you—if you choose to. Ask yourself: *Will finding a woman who will appreciate me be worth the change, work, and personal self-search I'll have to go through?* Am I willing to tackle this situation head-on?

How about after you put down this book? **Reading is one thing, doing is another.** If you don't choose to change, you will continue on the same path with the same problems.

"Things do not change, we change."
— Thoreau

"Me Tarzan,
You Jane."

—Edgar Rice Burroughs

Dominance 3
and
Protection

Before we go any further, please understand that women don't *plan* to mistreat you. They do not *revel* in watching you wince while they criticize you. In fact and this is a point which I can't stress enough, at an unconscious level, women hassle you <u>to see if you can fight back and to see what you are made of. They want you to stand up to them, they want you to be "the man."</u> This is the way it is.

This challenging of the male by the female is normal behavior for an *animal* that is protecting its territory. And how do animals behave when another animal threatens them? They fight back! They raise their hackles, fluff their feathers, or take a swipe at their challenger to show that they will fight to protect themselves. As human animals, we do the same thing. The female tests the male before she lets him touch her. A man who stands his ground with her can stand his ground against any other male who could potentially threaten her or her children. A man who doesn't let her push him around leaves her feeling safe, and she feels like offering herself to him even more. If the man with-draws, becomes suddenly "weak," or more commonly, stops giving her care and attention, the woman may stop having sex with him, and start her verbal attack. When she domi-nates the man this way, she becomes the stronger of the pair.

Each woman admires different traits in each man, depend-ing upon how she was socialized. However, after talking with hundreds of women and researching vast amounts of academic studies on mating, the basic characteristics women desire in a man appear to be universal:

1. Women are attracted to a man's <u>physical domi-nance</u> (his height and physical strength.)

2. Women are attracted to his <u>status </u>(his wealth and social position.) Before the industrial age came along in Western society, she was drawn to the hunter who brought home the best catch. The best hunter got the youngest and prettiest woman of the tribe by offering his meat to her.

3. Women want *protection* for their children. <u>Emo-tional nurturing</u>, which is crucial to her choice, is a form of protection for the mother and child. The man who will protect and provide for her during pregnancy gets his wife's devotion, and access to her sexual favors.

Every woman is attracted to some form of the above traits. <u>Intelligence</u> and <u>creativity</u> at work, can result in a higher income and thus improves status. A <u>good looking</u> man can attract a prettier woman and both sexes want to mate with someone better looking if they can; our children will be pret-tier as a result. If he's not good looking, money and wit are equal or even higher substitutions.

When animals mate, the female will choose the best male from those available in her territory. According to Charles

Darwin and other famous anthropologists, the female chooses the most genetically superior male, the male who can fend off all the other males and appears to be healthy. She notices his muscle tone and his stamina, his chest and his height. This is why taller, larger men have a genetic advantage over shorter men; unconsciously, their bodies send the message that they can physically protect the female. The male who appears "strong" sends this message through his positive self-image, and other non-verbal signals; he will not be overpowered. The female senses that *other men* are less likely to push him around and that she will be safe. The dominant male appears to be able to *protect* her. And so, she chooses the man who offers her a nice "nest" and the protection of his wing. . .

. . . and that is what women really want.

In <u>The Evolution of Desire</u>, Dr. David Buss tells of a male bird which builds a nest for the female. It sits in its nest and waits for a female to fly by. She stops, and inspects the nest by pulling and poking at the twigs and grass it is made from. If she finds it suitable, she stays and mates with him, if not, she flies on. After several females have vetoed the nest, the male pulls his nest apart and rebuilds it. How intelligent! This bird <u>does something</u> about its inability to attract the girl. It does not sit around like some humans do and feel hopeless about its odds.

I must stress that the female tendency to chose dominant men is unconscious, inherited from years of social conditioning and biologic destiny. Women don't stand around at cocktail parties thinking "I want to have kids with that guy; boy, does he have a great genetic pool." This selection pattern happens *automatically*, without the female being aware that she is doing it.

Kind men with gentle personalities offer us *emotional* protection. But remember that women will not view gentleness as a primary attraction unless it is coupled with dominant, assertive behavior. Unconsciously, we are still attracted to *dangerous* men, men who have an "edge." Sometimes the "dangerous" male looks outwardly aloof, obstinate or even "jerky." Sometimes he appears to have a dark, brooding side. He appears to withhold; he is a mystery. She has to work harder to attract him and if we have to work harder to get something, it appears to be more valuable. (This concept is a "universal influence technique"—see Chapter Eleven.) We are less likely to take him for granted; we are less likely to wander because we must also be on our toes to keep him in our territory.

This "dangerous" attitude is a front, a bluff to maintain his composure under fire. Underneath hides his vulnerability. <u>A truly attractive man must eventually show his vulnerable side and his ability to be a lover and a good father to her children.</u>

The more self-aware female will not stay with a man who is entirely "dangerous" or withholding for long. Ultimately he will need to offer her some emotional tenderness. Her intellect balances her attraction to the "dangerous" man. A woman who has waded through her share of "jerks" understands that "dangerous" behavior only goes so far to stimulate her. She also wants <u>emotional protection</u>, which a withholding man cannot offer. An insecure woman may find herself drawn to bad-boy behavior <u>due to misreading his withholding attitude as strength</u>, but the healthier female seeks a man who is *balanced*, a man who can be nurturing and still set his limits.

What is most important to remember is that initially, a female is attracted to a man who *appears to be strong*, a man she senses she will not have to protect. Yes, this statement is going to bother some people. However, in today's uncertain dating world **I teach what is real and what works.**

Listen, you can be right and be alone, or you can do what works, I am not implying that this is fair or "the way it should be." Mother nature doesn't favor fairness. She favors behavior that helps us to survive and procreate. Our civilized behavior masks the animal beneath. Talk to any social psychologist and read the research about what attracts each sex to the other. Now, you wouldn't argue that most men would rather have a younger, slender female would you? Well, face it, women have their preferences too.

According to scientific studies from thirty-seven countries and ten-thousand people, the female's biologic destiny of being the sex which carries the child explains her tendency to choose a supportive male who will stay with her throughout her pregnancy, protect and provide for her. Natural selection also explains why females are slower to become sexually aroused. Studies show that this lengthened arousal period allows the female more time to carefully choose the best male from those available to her. She cannot mate hastily, she has far more to lose than the male if she chooses a man who merely has sex, then bolts. An emotionally nurturing male is sexually patient; he can wait out the woman's ambivalence. He enjoys more extended foreplay and he also is more likely to gently hold her afterward and share intimate conversation.

Men have their hardwiring, too. Anthropologists attribute a male's tendency to roam, to get rapidly aroused by visual cues, and to want casual sex outside of the couple relationship to the biologic destiny of renewing our species. I used to think that if my husband ever had an affair, I would leave him. But after studying the mating history of many cultures, I began to see things from a different perspective. I became more tolerant of male behavior that feminists label "sexist," such as their attraction to younger women and their tendency to be promiscuous. I no longer blame men for being the way they are, although, as an "aging female," it's difficult not to get angry about mother nature's strategies. A man's tendency to mate visually is something that he can do very little about, though he may fight valiantly to resist these urges. "Exceptionally few" men would resist choosing a young, beautiful female if they could attract her, all things being equal.

After years of working with countless men and women's mating behavior, watching older men choose younger women at parties, and listening to women privately tell me which men they are attracted to (yes, the taller, well-dressed ones with confidence and money), I am convinced that unconscious, biologic destiny is at work. To what extent societal conditioning shapes these ancient urges we do not know. In scientific circles, it is a hotly debated topic called "nature versus nurture."

Feminists, for example believe that the male tendency to choose younger women is due to our sexist culture which objectifies the female body. They say the older male—younger female courtship is due to middle-aged male insecurity. But evolutionary psychologists attribute male choice to mother nature's need to perpetuate the species, for the younger the woman is, the more likely she is to conceive.

Certainly, economy plays a large role in sexual strategy. Remember that women still earn less money for equal work than men do and that single mothers often have financial difficulty; this makes mating both a romantic and a financial proposition.

Most women with children appreciate the cushion of an extra paycheck. Even if she does have a good job, or earns as much or more than he does, she must take time off for delivery. Rising housing, daycare, education, health care and parenting costs make the more affluent male a much more desirable choice. Many child-free women have less financial difficulty, but still enjoy <u>the feeling</u> if not the actual need for security that the affluent male offers. That is why one of the first things a woman wants to know about a man is what he does for a living. For example, a man says to his buddy:

"Last night I had a date with
this outrageous looking redhead."

While a woman comments to
her girlfriend:

"Last night I had a date with
this well-known lawyer."

Note how the different sexes initially describe their dates. Both desire a high status mate. A male sees high status in her beauty and youth; a female sees it through his financial worth and social influence.

Rule: High status equals high mating desirability

These first filtering devices: status, physical strength or height and an assertive attitude are what I call "the gatekeepers." If the man we are considering does not possess some of these qualities, he may not get past the first gate to dating us. These characteristics are not the only criteria we select from, but they are the most critical

Civilization and shifting social conditions have caused women to reconsider some of their traditional mating habits. In the past twenty years, women have found their place in the world of work. It is clear this new power position is beginning to have deep and far-reaching ramifications for the way we mate. For example, research shows that women don't find marriage as appealing as it was fifty years ago when they were raised to be mothers and housewives. In fact, the more money a woman has, the less likely she is to view marriage as a desirable state. Affluent single women have little reason to choose a mate based on financial status. Women with the emotional strength and smarts to stand as individuals are asking for more intangible qualities in a man, qualities such as kindness, flexibility, sensitivity and spirituality.

The new requests women made of men back in the sixties started the communication problems we are now struggling with. As women gained power in the world of work, and learned that there was more to life than being a wife and mother, they became more assertive. This confused a lot of men; believe me, it confused a lot of women too. Because of male reaction to feminism, women got more than they bargained for. Ironically, confronted by the independent woman, men who were socialized in the sixties, seventies and even the eighties pulled back their power. They stopped being assertive, and instead started to follow or acted **noncommittal.** They let women lead in order to please them and they are miserable about doing it. Women don't like it either, and agree that men are acting overly meek.

Because in America it is no longer OK to be a macho, old world male, men are searching for a new identity. But many men have confused "sensitive" behavior with submissive, doormat behavior. And when men act submissive, women retaliate with criticism. Because they dislike being pushed around, but are forbidden from reacting physically (which is an instinctual response when we are threatened), many men act out their anger through "passive-aggressive" behavior. That is, they *appear* to go along with the woman's lead, but sabotage the relationship by holding secret grudges, becoming less communicative and most significantly withdrawing commitment.

This **indirect** behavior *is driving women crazy.* We are on the warpath looking for some "real men," because we aren't attracted to and don't respect passive behavior. We wonder, **where have all the MEN gone?** Unfortunately, many of us continue to alienate men by emasculating and belittling them. (If men talked about women the way most women bad-mouth men, they'd <u>never</u> get away with it!) But, please understand these misguided communications:

> *What we are actually trying to do is to get men to take back their strength.*

Women have to allow men be men—to stop trying to make men into something they are not. Men grunt, sweat, swear, get moody and don't continuously "have their feelings" about everything. Men need to learn to set limits without becoming hostile and abusive; <u>they need to learn the middle ground, the balance point between being a doormat or a jerk.</u>

Most of the women I work with who are fairly healthy really do not want the distancing jerk. They want a man with balance; a balanced man does not give his power away by becoming overly accommodating or passive, or withholding his affection and pulling away. But balance is not easy to learn, especially when you have been brought up to behave a certain way, and have related to women that way for years.

The female's unconscious need for protection is a partial explanation for the actions of women who have gone for long periods of time without mates. These women often appear defensive and tough. This attitude shows up in "male bashing." *Not exactly an attractive way to get closer to you, huh guys?* However, these women have lots of reasons to guard themselves; women without mates have to defend themselves both financially and physically. Unconsciously and justifiably <u>they harden themselves against adversity</u>. They put on psychological armoring in order to get by in this lonely and physically dangerous world—<u>just like the loner male</u>. And often, they have been hurt. They remember being vulnerable once too often, they remember being left when they showed their softer side. Sound familiar?

You may be interested to know that the men I work with who appear cool and aloof often feel quite shy and awkward inside. Their brilliant defense strategy, acting like a jerk, acting as if they don't care, protects them. Underneath this front lies the soft underbelly of a somewhat insecure, very human guy.

The independent woman behaves in a similar manner. This self-sufficient female is cautious when a man approaches. Is he interesting enough to risk giving up her hard-earned freedom? What can he offer? Why should she let down her guard?

For she has no other guard but herself!

And so, she tests him. This testing maneuver is a double-edged sword. The independent, often well-educated and financially secure female appears to be a "challenge." Can he tame her? However, she can also be "high maintenance." Sadly, many women alienate men before giving them a chance to shine. Because she doesn't show her softer, feminine side until she feels safe, she appears too threatening and "difficult." She can't accept him right away due to her self-reliant defense, so he moves on.

Tired of the uphill battle this challenging woman offers, many men do choose the path of least resistance, the traditional, compliant and often passive female they feel important around. This choice makes perfect sense. The submissive female makes him feel strong and in control, something an insecure man may desperately need. He may even get the chance to rescue her, which makes him feel even more in command. But, he also tires quickly of this emotionally helpless victim. Is it any surprise that women also quickly tire around "nice guys?"

Strong women who can take care of themselves also want to feel feminine, and soft. They get tired of playing "superwoman." In order to allow their softer side to emerge, these women need to feel that occasionally, *they* can lean on some-

one. <u>A kind, gentle man who cannot also exhibit a strong,</u>
<u>take-charge, leanable side does not appear to be powerful</u>
<u>enough to handle *her* burdens.</u>

> *For instinctually, women are not*
> *attracted to men they have to lead.*

Initially, the nice guy/doormat who doesn't push back *does*
seem pleasant to be with after encountering the distant, un-
reliable jerk. But a nice guy without a good dose of dominance and assertiveness, a man we can't feel safe to lean
on will eventually bore *us* and we have no choice but to
move on.

"Failure: the path
of least persistence."

—*Anon*

Why You Are Not Attracting Women and What to Do About It

4

There are many reasons why you are not attracting or keeping women. From a female perspective, I will give you an idea of why this may be happening. Below I list ten major turn-offs to women. Don't be alarmed if you have one of them. Read what you can do about them and take action!

1. You don't have a job that pays as well as the one we have.

2. You are more than ten years older than we are or you look that way.

3. You are not as tall as we are or taller.

4. You are more than twenty pounds over your ideal weight or, you have a noticeable "pot."

5. You smoke and/or you drink excessively or use drugs.

6. You are wearing a toupee or doing "the comb-over."

7. You are quiet, unassuming and/or overly nice.

8. You have poor hygiene and/or dress like a nerd.

9. You cannot talk about your needs, desires or any feelings you have about our relationship.

10. You fall into the jerk category— you can't let us get close to you; you are emotionally unavailable or you are using us for sex.

Other minor league turn-offs that you could possibly be creating:

1. You live at home with your parents.

2. You have a nasal voice, nervous laughter or self-deprecating behavior.

3. You can't tear yourself away from the TV or sports channel; you spend the majority of your time in front of the video or the internet.

4. You are cheap and regularly ask us to go dutch or worse, borrow money.

5. You call us "babe" and "honey" when you've just met us.

6. You don't know how to take it slow sexually or you have other sexual problems that interfere, like addiction to 900 numbers or rapid ejaculation (which you haven't tried to take care of.)

7. You have noticeable, sprouting hair plugs.

8. You cannot carry on a conversation. You become quiet.

9. You wear gold chains, loud jewelry. Or, you wear tight shirts which you unbutton to show your chest hair. This is especially a turn-off to educated women.

10. Your obviously dyed dark hair contrasts with your pale skin (a la Ronald Reagan.)

11. You wear synthetic ties, cheap clothing, or cheap accessories. Your clothes don't go well together, or they are dirty or wrinkled.

12. You drive a beat-up junker car that is dirty.

13. You are terminally messy (to a neatnick it's *awful*, to a messy women, a vast relief).

14. You come on too strong or talk about our bodies or overly personal subjects too soon.

15. You reveal all the skeletons in your closet before we've had a chance to warm up to you. "Hello, I'm in recovery!" Where do we go from there?

16. You stand too close when you meet us and don't give us room to check you out. No woman wants a man she doesn't know to stand close.

17. You talk about your custody battles with your ex and how awful she was, how she's taken you to the cleaners. We can't help but think *we might be next.*

18. You swear a lot in front of us. "**#*this, *^#*that. This is not polite or well-bred.

19. Your eyes roam over our bodies when you look at us.

20. You stare at us fixedly. This is rude and weird. Maybe you're not aware that you do this?

21. You talk about all the other women who are "hitting on you" to try to impress us. It doesn't.

22. You boast overtly about the KIND of EXPENSIVE car you drive. Or, you name drop.

23. You have no sense of humor.

24. You don't open doors for us, and you walk through before us. You drive off before making sure our car starts. In short, you have no manners.

There are several other obvious turn-offs, such as you have just been released from prison, you collect large balls of lint, and last, but certainly not least:

. . . **You are married,** (even if you *are* really, really, really going to get a divorce.) However, if you *are* married, you can eliminate this problem by dating a sweet, caring, easily influenced woman. First, lie to your girlfriend and tell her that you are not really married. When she finds out, tell her you are *going* to leave your wife and marry her if she will *only be patient* enough—this should get her in the sack! Finally, but most importantly, *after you have spent years with her,* tell her that you have decided to make a go of it with your wife "for the kid's sake." She will understand. I'm sure John Bobbitt did.

LET'S EXAMINE THE TOP TEN TURN-OFFS LIST:

1) Money

Women usually date and marry men of their own socio-economic level or higher. Remember, in our culture, status = power = $. It will be very difficult for you to attract a woman if you make considerably less money than she does. Money is the single most powerful bargaining tool that you have as a man. It's worth going back to school and getting a degree for, and worth all the hassle that it brings if you want to attract desirable women. Why do you see beautiful women with average looking (and sometimes much shorter) men? Because these men have money, and the power that it brings.

> (Gentlemen, this does not make us "gold-diggers!" Are you a jerk because you would prefer to be with younger, slender women? Of course not, it's the way you are wired. You mate visually; we mate for protection.)

As I mentioned earlier, some exceptions to the rule of women choosing men with money concern extremely handsome men who have no money whatsoever. These types can often attract women who will take care of them financially (much like the "kept" woman). You will also occasionally see an older, less attractive woman who is wealthy with a younger man who is not. Both of them are doing "the trade-off" as well.

What to do about it:

Go back to school. Get trained. Get into computers or some other lucrative field. You're going to be thirty-five, forty or fifty anyway. . .why not follow that dream?

2) Age

Ten years younger is OK (provided you have *some* sort of personality and are not a teenager), but we are wary of you-if you marry us, you might leave when we get older for a younger woman who can have babies. If you *look* more than ten years older than we do, we will not find you attractive, especially if we have managed to stay looking younger than our age. If we can mate with a male who is our age—we will do it. Usually men look for women ten years younger than they are, and women look for men five years younger to five years older. If you *are* ten years older than we are and don't look it, that's all that matters. No, you don't have to lie about your age. Remember, if you have other bargaining points, money, status, height, a vocabulary, the ability to dance, we may be willing to date you *despite* how old you are. Now you know how women *your* age feel, darling!

What to do about it

If you look a lot younger than you are, say, you're thirty and you look twenty-five, make sure the girl knows it as soon as possible. Comb your hair off your forehead to look more sophisticated. Do not wear "boyish" clothes like colored tennis shoes, multi-colored hip jackets or MTV sweatshirts. You'll look younger. Think elegant. Wear a sports jacket with slacks. No T-shirts. Wear a black leather jacket, beautiful leather loafers and think cool.

If you look older than you are—you may appear this way because:

- You are wearing a mustache AND a beard AND glasses. You are hiding your face! Shave it off and try to get contacts.

Attention all men: Did you know that ninety percent of all women prefer a clean-shaven man at any age? Now you do.

- The dye job looks bad. Get it done professionally. Nothing spells nerd like a home bottle dye job (except maybe a rug.)
- You've been out in the sun or you've lost a lot of weight and your facial skin is sagging. Consider plastic surgery or collagen injections; if I told you would attract younger women if you did would it be worth your while? See the index for a great plastic surgeon.
- Your clothes are dated. Wear jeans to look younger. Wear the muti-colored jacket! Avoid black and other drab colors. Dark colors drain the youth out of your face.
- Smile! This takes off five years instantly.
- Your glass frames haven't been updated in years. Stop being so practical and go buy new ones. It is boring and doormatish to wear the same pair year after year.
- You haven't been exercising. Exercise! Besides, exercise releases testosterone and you know what THAT does.

3) Height

Sorry, but it's the hard truth. A guy that's taller than she is can make her feel secure. This is a sexy feeling to a woman. If you are as tall as we are, we're not going to find this unattractive, but we do notice it and wish you were taller. In this case, it'll help to have additional bargaining points, a stellar personality or a great job to give yourself stature. If you are shorter than we are, it will be extremely helpful for you to have more bargaining points. And please, stop beating yourself over the head about it! Running around feeling crummy doesn't help. Get counseling for your negative attitude and develop your other great selling points. What's "short?" Anything less than three inches taller than we are. If you are under 5'7," you would be considered short even by the majority of American women who are 5'4 - 5'7".

What to do about it

- Always approach the woman when she is sitting and you can stand or lean; you'll look taller. Stand up as straight as possible. Take a look at her shoes. She's wearing heels? You're in luck. She's shorter than she appears to be. Believe me, women know about height problems. Remember that tall women (over 5'8") need to bargain too. That's because the average male is 5'9 1/2". A tall girl is used to being with men her height.

- Buy some height enhancing shoes. See the shoe reference in the resource section. No kidding. Cowboy boots with heels work well too. Women wear push-up bras, why shouldn't you help yourself out, too?

- Wear clothes that are all in one tone. Beige pants, beige shirt, neutral belt. Wearing two colors will visually cut your height down. A dark color on top will make your chest look smaller. You don't need to look smaller. Ever! I don't care if every other guy is wearing black. If you are shorter, you wear white or light colors. See Chapter Nine.

- Wear shoes that have long lines. Do not wear shoes with straps, laces, buckles or any leather piece that cuts horizontally across the top of the foot.

- Avoid tight collars and round necks. Especially if you are carrying weight. A "v" neck will make you appear taller, as well as vertically striped shirts. Wear horizontally striped shirts to broaden, especially on the shoulders

Seek and date shorter women if you want to date more regularly. This may mean going to places where Asian or Latin women go. It means searching the room for the shortest woman there; the girl you will look taller around. It means responding to personal ads of women who are three inches shorter than you are. Remember, just saying you like tall women doesn't mean they like shorter men. It's not good news, but it's real.

4) Weight

<u>Yes, this bugs us too</u>— but not as much as *our* weight bothers *you*. It's the "pot" we don't like. Carrying weight isn't a deal breaker so work out and distribute it.

<u>What to do about it</u>

- If you do have a pot, don't cinch your belt under it and wear tight shirts and a big belt buckle. This makes it look worse; a big belt buckle in the center of a big stomach only draws attention to it. Yuck! Cover it up. Cultivate the over-hanging oversized shirt look.

- Avoid wearing white on the top, as well as wearing horizontal stripes which makes you appear larger. Wear darker colors, and avoid loud colors, splashy patterns and wide ties.

- If you have a combination of thinning hair, a pot and are on the short side, do something about what you *can* change. A general rule is, if we are overweight, we will be willing to go out with you if you are too. But if we are thin and you are obviously fatter (not just ten pounds) chances are it turns us off.

5) Addiction

You've heard it a hundred times by now. Women who are not addicted to what you are will not find you attractive. Yes, we *can* smell the alcohol on your breath! Did you know that if you are an alcoholic you are more likely to be lacking a certain enzyme in your blood? People who are not alcoholics do have this element which breaks down and helps the blood stream absorb alcohol. So when an alcoholic drinks, he smells of it right away due to his body's inability to synthesize it. An enlarged nose, and/or your constant need to drink gives you away too. Smokers: The smoke in your clothes is immediately noticeable and you taste terrible when we kiss you. Stick with the smokers if you smoke and try not to take offense if we won't go out with you. Even if you smoke a little, eventually the issue will come up.

As to other addictions, I once went out with a man who proudly told me he was sober and never drank any more. I congratulated him on his recovery, then asked him if he had any other regular habits. Oh yes, he replied, he smoked grass almost every day. That was the last he saw of me.

What to do about it

Refrain from smoking on the days you are planning to look for women. Wear a newly laundered outfit so you won't smell like smoke. Use breath mints. For alcoholics, try putting a sign on your wall that says:

Which is more important—
a woman or my drinking?

Look, you don't have to be pure to attract women. But remember, like attracts like. If you want to attract higher functioning women, you have to be higher functioning yourself. YOU KNOW WHO YOU ARE. Get help or stop complaining about your love life.

6) Baldness

OK, Here's the truth. At first, if you are very, totally, or just-a fringe-left-bald, we aren't going to drop dead at your feet. But! <u>That's only if you are under thirty-five</u>, because most men under thirty-five have most of their hair. If you're over thirty-five, and you've got an assertive attitude and like yourself, we may not notice it at all. But for the record, according to recent research and straw polls of the women I talk with, <u>only about one-fourth of all women are turned off by balding men</u>. Feel better?

What we definitely *hate* are comb-overs and toupees! I have only met one undetectable toupee. And that was worn by one of the wealthiest plastic surgeons in the United States (his nurse told me.) Every other toupee is out. <u>We spend the entire evening thinking about it and looking at it.</u> *We can't even concentrate on the conversation we're having with you it's so obvious.* (Haven't you *noticed* how our eyes keep drifting up?) A truly non-noticeable toupee will put you back a couple thousand easily, and you'll still have to take it off eventually.

What to do about it

Take your rug off now. . . . Whew! Everyone will thank you for it. Comb your remaining hair straight back, or shave it off. Guys look sexy when they're bald. See Dr. Ely's discussion in Chapter Nine.

- An interesting note. I had a client who told me that when he began wearing his rug, the people in the office all said it looked nice. OK, it <u>was</u> a fairly decent one. But I ask you, <u>what were his co-workers going to do, tell him that he shouldn't have done it?</u> Because it was obvious that he was suddenly wearing one, the *polite* thing to do was to compliment him, but the *honest* thing would have been to tell him the truth! An example of this that you can relate to is when a woman cuts her hair and says to you—"How do you like it?" Do you say—"It looks awful?" No, you lie! So, please guys, get the hint.

- There are other surgical options, like cutting a flap of the hair that's still growing, wrapping it around and stitching it onto the balding area. I suggest that before you have any other strange procedures done that you meet face to face with a guy who has already taken the plunge. Take a woman with you and have her inspect whatever it is that you are considering. If she can detect it—forget it. Do not rely on filmed examples or pictures.

About plugs. Ditto. For the average Joe who only can afford a few thousand dollars, these things look like hell. They can distract even the most fascinating conversation. The cheap jobs look like CARROTS are sprouting up there. Remember—if *you* see them, we do too.

Your *attitude* about yourself can transcend any physical shortcomings you have. When you think of all the balding men who are considered to be attractive, it's their *confidence* that makes them sexy. Develop your other strengths. And make sure that you don't have the double whammy of being bald <u>and</u> overweight; this ages you a great deal. Add short and you really need to get some other bargaining tools on your side. Remember that women have these troubles too. Balding, short men can still find wives, but fifty-five-year-old overweight women have a much harder time of it. Balding is acceptable and normal. Get over it.

7) You are overly nice

See Chapter Two and re-read it.

What to do about it

- Get counseling for your co-dependency and low self-esteem. Set limits and say no!
- Take an assertiveness training class.

- Get a small spiral notebook. Keep track of every time you say yes when you mean no, or let yourself get taken advantage of by <u>anyone</u>. **You are responsible for the way people treat you.**

- Practice talking loud. Get a tape recorder, count to ten (1-2-3-4-5 etc.) at what you now think is a "5" in volume. Then count to ten again at what you think is a "7," on up until you get to "10" as the loudest. Do this daily, and see if you can progressively get your "10" voice to be louder. See if you can get people around you to ask why you are talking so loud. <u>Passive men are almost always soft-spoken.</u>

The Most Effective Way to Lose Doormat Behavior:

If you were playing baseball and wanted to hit a home run, where would you aim? Second base? Center field? NO! Out of the park, that's where. This is the "over shooting" concept. You aim for being a jerk, and with a little luck you will land just over the zero point on the doormat-jerk scale.

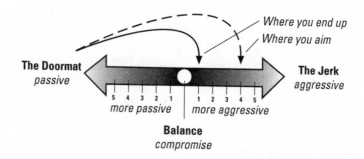

You'll probably end up closer to "balance" if you overshoot, because you are already so nice that even though <u>you</u> may think you are being far too nasty, you are in all probability being normal. You are used to being pushed around, so you can't accurately gage how you are coming across. Far better for someone to accuse you of being a jerk than a wimp! So make that your goal, AIM FOR BEING A JERK. When some woman (finally) says you are being terrible, you have come a long way, baby!

8) Hygiene
See Chapter Nine

9 and 10) You cannot talk about your feelings for us and/ or you may be acting like a jerk

These are not mutually inclusive items, but often seem to show up in the same guy. A shy man may not be able to talk about his feelings because he is tongue-tied. The "jerk" really has no immediate interest in anything other than himself. <u>I cannot stress strongly enough that you must be able to talk to a woman about how you feel about her</u>. You *don't* want to overwhelm her with your undying love, that is doormatdom. But, you *do* want to tell her she means a lot to you so that she won't think you are taking her for granted. Expensive dinners and gifts are nice, but there are other, more important things a woman needs.

What to do about it

- Follow this rule. If she is quieter than you are, if you quiet down too, she may open up and talk. This is called <u>mirroring</u> (see Chapter Seven.) If you are acting like a doormat (you can figure this out, because she is acting nonchalant), chattering away at her *won't* work. Cultivate balance. Don't *always* tell her she is beautiful, but sometimes you must. Don't *always* talk about your feelings, but do consistently show her you care. She must not think you are a pushover. Read Chapter Eleven and use the brilliant and deadly influence technique <u>intermittent reinforcement.</u>
- You must <u>say the words</u> "You are important to me" or "I feel so good when I am around you." "You are so beautiful" *always* works wonders. Use <u>feeling</u>

words; "I <u>feel</u> so good when I am around you," or "I <u>feel</u> really close to you." Avoid the word "love" until you really mean it; we may take you at your word, an intriguing concept. Review Chapter Six about talking.

- <u>Getting over being selfish means taking an accurate and brutal personal inventory</u>. Are you getting anywhere in your relationship life? Have you been progressively able to sustain better relationships as you have aged? This is a good sign. No?...Is your main gripe that women keep wanting to settle down and you don't? Do you have them waiting in the wings for you? Do most women bore you? Do you seek CHALLENGES? Uh-Oh. You may be a jerk! You may be looking for that one girl who treats you as coolly as you have treated most women. What's the answer here? Get thee to a good therapist who you are NOT able to fool. Preferably, a man who you think is a bit of a jerk, too

OTHER THINGS WOMEN PAY ATTENTION TO

When a woman is out "hunting" for men, she surreptitiously surveys the room for men she finds attractive. You may be interested to know what most women immediately scan for. She may eliminate you from her hunt (or find you interesting) due to the following visual signals:

1. <u>Your hair.</u> Is it long or short?

- **A ponytail or long hair** signals you as "hip" or "artistic" or "Fabio" (if you're young and beautifully built), but it ages a man who is over thirty-five and looks it.

- **The comb-over** signals nerdy, desperate and older.

- **Shorter hair** says you are more conventional and more youthful.

- **Gray hair** signals distinction and often, money.

2. <u>Signs of age</u>. Many women do *not* want to go out with younger men; we are over our fertile years. If you are a great deal younger, and haven't had children, chances are you may leave us eventually to marry someone you can have children with. So, we look for graying temples and laugh lines. Sometimes women even eliminate men who may be their age because they look <u>too</u> young. If this describes you, let the woman know how old you are as soon as tactfully possible.

3. <u>Higher-class dressing.</u> When in doubt, wear a tie and nice shoes. Buy fewer items if you can't afford a lot and spend more on what you do buy.

4. <u>Wedding rings.</u> The smart female huntress looks for this immediately, as well as ring marks.

5. <u>Your car and the way you take care of it.</u>

6. <u>Your kids and how often you see them.</u> If you are a good dad and make time to see them she'll be impressed. She watches how you talk to them, and if you show love and concern for them. If your children take first place over dating her, she may need more attention and pout, which is a good way to screen your dates for needy women. She should be willing to share equal time with them. If your work and the kids are taking up more time than the time you spend with her, and you <u>want</u> to date her, make more time or she may leave. Note: Do NOT let your date sit in the back seat when you are all driving somewhere, even if she offers to and your child begs for the front. This will put her second and your children get the message that they can control you both.

7. <u>Your ex and how you treat her.</u> Do you snarl and swear under your breath every time you mention your ex? Your date will wonder why you ever got involved with such a dysfunctional woman, is there something about YOU that maybe she should watch out for? It's OK to sigh with resignation, but for the first few months, keep your bitterness to yourself. Get counseling if your anger is interfering with your ability to parent your kids.

Although you may have been taken to the cleaners by your ex, we cannot be held responsible for your dirty laundry

---

8. <u>Putting your arm around other women.</u> We wonder— are you with her? Or are you a jerk and just schmoozing? We *don't* think that you are a hell of an attractive and popular guy if you are putting your arm around other women. And never, *ever* put your arm around a woman or touch her other than to shake hands when you are just getting to know her. The most you can get away with is squeezing her arm if you're a touchy-feely type. But if the purpose of your touch is to move in—we feel it. A well-bred woman will back away and resent you for this.

9. <u>A gloomy, morose look.</u> This could intrigue us or turn us off, depending upon our psychological health. However, you can never go wrong with a pleasant smile.

10. <u>Your ability to dance.</u> No matter how little money you have or your lack of height, if you can partner dance you will have dates. Learn the waltz, fox-trot, swing and some Latin. A side note: please don't try to pull her close when you barely know her into an intimate slow dance. Her resistance is because you are moving way too fast.

11. <u>Your knowledge of the social circle</u> you are both involved in.

12. <u>Your social "title" or function</u> at the event where she meets you. Are you the president? Then wear a name tag that says so or tell her. It's OK to be important now and then.

13. <u>Your athletic ability</u> at sporting events.

14. The general energy tone you carry. Are you lively and up? Good. Are you low and down? Bad.

15. A "macho" attitude. This always looks phony. Your insecurity is spelled out loud and clear. Do not mistake "macho" for strong. Strong is direct, level and clear. Macho is boasting, swaggering your body around, overly loud talking, insecure and reactive.

16. A selfish attitude. Because you are insecure, because you have been hurt in the past, you are keeping your toys to yourself. You are afraid to go the extra inch. You don't drive to pick her up; instead, you try to get her to meet you halfway so you don't have to drive too far. You want her to pay half the ticket to the show; you expect her to be quiet while you listen to the game in the car or while you practice your putting. Only a meek, victimy woman will follow these orders, not a woman who has self-esteem. And don't get upset when she doesn't call you, and say, "The phone works both ways you know." Understand courtship. Yes, she would rather have you call her. And yes, I've asked women under thirty how they feel about this. Over three-fourths of them want YOU to call. Yes, this is called jumping through hoops. . . . and it's also called foreplay! You'll have to work hard for the best women.

17. Your intelligence and general knowledge of the world. Depending upon how educated she is, she wants to carry on a conversation with a man who can talk about interesting things: politics, philosophy, definitely psychology and yes, the "f" word—FEELINGS. So read. Read *The Wall Street Journal*. Read bestsellers. Follow market trends. Take evening courses.

18. What are your hobbies and are they like hers? Let her know what they are, take her out and teach her how to do them. You do have hobbies don't you? You should have at least two BESIDES THE INTERNET to make yourself interesting.

19. Your upper body definition. She won't notice if you don't have it (unless your upper body is extremely small,) but if you do have a well-developed chest, it will turn her on. If you are slender, work out, get nutritional advice and put some weight on.

20. Your manners and your use of chivalry. See Chapter Five.

21. Your ethnic background. OK, this is a touchy subject, but here's the truth. In the real world, women are attracted to men who are in the "dominant culture." In western society, this means white males. If you aren't white, you are going to have to look harder— a lot harder to date white women. It is still the case that ONLY THE EXCEPTIONAL WOMAN will date and marry outside of her race. It is also the case that most white men want to date white women— except for Latin or Asian women which many do like.

- Like attracts like. Genetic selection keeps us from mating with people who will dilute or redistribute our gene pool unless some unknown buzzer goes off inside of us telling us to cross-mate to improve our group. For example, all races have a built in switch telling us to mate with people who are more attractive than we are so that our children will be more attractive. But the switch that allows us to cross racial lines has not been thrown in most people.

If you are a Middle Easterner, Asian, or African American, you are going to need to have MAJOR bargaining tools to attract white women. This means height and money, and a western attitude and dress. It means Americanizing your accent. Go to the white, upper-middle class department stores like *Nordstrom* and *Eddie Bauer*. Tell the clerks that you want to dress like most young white guys do. Get rid of all your black leather clothes, turbans, beads and rasta regalia. White guys can wear black leather clothes, but it makes a dark-skinned guy look darker. Think mainstream. It works. Like I have said—this isn't the way it should be, but it's the way it is. You can be right and alone if you want, or you can adapt.

Your other alternative is to date women from your own ethnic background. You don't want to do this? Examine your motivation. Is there something about your ethnic background you are ashamed of? This attitude will also be unappealing. Learn to accept what is real, and work to add to, not hide your family roots.

WHAT TO AVOID DOING ON A DATE

1. Leering at other women. Especially those who are younger and thinner than your date. We are quick to notice your eyes wandering. We have eagle eyes and the peripheral vision of a hammerhead shark.

2. Making comments about the breasts, legs, or physical goodies of other women. Zip it!

3. Making jokes to cover up your nervousness. Just try your best to spit it out; we aren't going to bite you. We understand nervousness, but stand-up comedy is pathetic.

4. Making sexually explicit jokes—"exceptionally few" women will tolerate this. Test the waters before you launch into one.

5. Telling racially biased jokes. Again, only the exceptional woman will enjoy being politically incorrect. What is NOT OK is to put others down because you are uncomfortable about yourself.

6. Watching TV when you are out with us at a sports bars. Especially if the relationship has not progressed far enough to warrant this lack of interest. If it's the play-offs, avoid struggle and make your plans for another evening. We don't always have to have your complete attention, but once

every three minutes is nice.

7. Driving silently home. For that matter, driving silently anywhere as we chatter away. What is he thinking, we wonder? Are we making idiots of ourselves? You must keep the ball going a bit to avoid possible misconceptions about your silence. The ONLY time it is all right to stay silent for a long time is when you use it purposefully as an influence technique after you have given too much, and you want to create some mystery to regain the balance of power.

TO SUM UP THE MAIN REASONS YOU AREN'T ATTRACTING WOMEN

1. You are aiming way too high to begin with. She's not attracted to you because you aren't in her league.OR:

2. You have personal habits which turn her off.OR:

3. You have a very low opinion of yourself, and even if you are a match for her, she is turned off by your negative attitude. GET COUNSELING.

A QUICK WAY TO TELL WHETHER YOUR PROBLEM IS POOR PERSONAL HABITS OR AIMING TOO HIGH

Consider the points below. Are you a match in the following areas?

1. **Income**

   I make more than she does or at least as much.

2. **Height**

   I as tall or taller than she is.

3. **Weight**

   I am in relatively as good shape as she is. I am not more overweight than she is.

4. **Looks**

She is not more than "one point" above me in looks.

5. **Education**

I have the same education as she does, or higher.

6. **Class**

We are both white collar or we are both blue collar. If there is a difference, I am of the "higher" class, (women "mate up").

7. **Race**

We are of the same race. If there is a difference, she is of the "less dominant" culture.

8. **Personal style and energy level**

She seems to match me in energy and attitude. I am not more depressed or unhappy than she is.

If you said yes to six out of the eight categories, you are well-matched. If she's not attracted to you, you need to improve your self-esteem and social skills and get more of a life so you don't become a doormat.

Figuring out what is getting in your way is hard, I know. Start by eliminating things you know aren't a problem. Then deal with your clothes. (Read Chapter Nine and do a wardrobe overhaul.) Pay the personal shopper at the store to dress you. Your mother is biased. If you have a female friend who dates regularly, pay her to dress you. This is not the same as "getting your colors done" which women get excited by but you don't need. If you think that clothes aren't your problem (although I know very few non-daters who dress well), move on to social skills such as how to talk with a woman, body language and learning how to go at a woman's dating and sexual pace. You can do it. I think I can I think I can. . .

"Chivalry: the deportment
of a man toward any
woman not his wife."

—*Anon*

Behavior That Attracts Women

5

I have observed the mating behavior of both sexes for many years. At large gatherings, I see which men attract the most women; I ask women what they would like men to do more of, do less of or not do at all. Women have definite patterns of choosing men, and most of these patterns repeat consistently. The men who learn *and put into action* the behaviors that women prefer are the men who attract women rapidly. On the following pages, I list the most common behaviors which women find attractive. Some are well-known, but not always used; some are secrets that women know, but don't share with men. These techniques are grounded in solid behavioral psychology. The theory behind each technique is taught at nearly every self-improvement seminar in existence. I can assure you both as a professional and as a woman, they work.

In Chapter Eleven I discuss universal techniques which attract both sexes. If you don't seem to be having luck, you probably don't know some basic techniques. Many of these facts are not covered in other books, simply because most men do not buy self-improvement books, so there aren't many books written about men's problems available. In the Resource Section, I list several excellent books that can expand your knowledge about women, mating, sexuality and personal relationships.

Just *reading* this book is not going to do you any good. I mention this several times. You must <u>act</u> on new knowledge. Improvement and success are not spectator sports.

If you are bound and determined *not* to meet women, don't practice any of the techniques I offer, question them all, intellectualize and stall for time. But first, decide how much longer you want to be alone.

WHAT WORKS WITH WOMEN

1. Always tell her she is beautiful. *Never, ever tell her she has fat thighs or is overweight.* She already knows it! *Never* reinforce her negative view of herself. If she asks you if you think she is fat, tell her that you love who *she* is, and that whether she is large or small is merely icing on the cake. This is hopefully a truthful statement which won't cause her additional pain. Or, ask her why she is worrying about it. She will probably say that she's overweight. Don't let her bait you into agreeing with her. Just say that you will support her decision when she decides she wants to lose weight.

A reminder gentlemen, women who gain weight are not dealing with their personal problems. They are unhappy and literally stuffing it. If you were involved with a slender woman and she gained weight *after* you got together, <u>you are most definitely a part of the problem</u>. If you want a thinner girlfriend, listen and try to give her what she needs. Ask her if there is anything you are doing which is making her unhappy. Adding fuel to the fire by criticizing her will make her feel even worse and cause her to eat more. Instead of complaining about her weight, take her exercising, hiking, and subtly keep her away from high calorie foods and cheese-loaded restaurants. Talk about *your* weight, and how you are trying to lose it.

Only have a serious talk with her about how important it would be to you if she lost weight if you have decided that you will leave her unless she loses it. Tell her the way you feel, and that you're sorry you are so hung up on looks. Add that you realize that this is your problem, and that you have tried to change to no avail. Say, "It's my fault." (Arnie Becker, the sleazy lawyer on LA Law, used to advise men to do this too. Unfortunately or fortunately, however you are ethically inclined, it works.) Maybe if you are honest about your fixation she won't leave and she'll lose weight. . .but I doubt it.

People who focus on the outside, who need to have beautiful people around them are trying to boost their own low self-esteem by hanging around with those who will make them look good by association. It is called "the halo effect." We hope that if we stand next to these beautiful beings, their halo will shed light upon us too.

If your girlfriend leaves you and tells you that it is because *you've* gotten fat or lost your hair, this is her problem. Clearly, who *you* are is less important to her than how you look.

However, a mate's exterior appearance *is* crucial to sex appeal. In fact, sex appeal can disappear if the initial, visual triggers no longer operate to keep a couple close. The person who is primarily visual will have a hard time being attracted to someone who is overweight, messy or not good looking. Despite the intellectual knowledge that they should not judge on exteriors, these people still find it hard to adapt to an unattractive mate. As a man I am sure you can relate to this visual mating issue. If your girlfriend has lost her beauty, it is up to you to decide when and if you will draw the line and have that often final serious talk. Before you do, try everything possible to support her without becoming critical.

2. Do detective work. Discover what she believes no one appreciates about her personality, figure out what her hidden, less than obvious strengths are. Let her know that you *do* appreciate her for them. For example, admire how hard she tries, how wonderful it is that she is so *emotional* (even if it scares the hell out of you), or her artistic ability. If she has a beautiful figure, talk about how smart she is. If she is well-educated, compliment her on her beauty. Learn the obvious, then compliment her on what isn't so obvious. (This is also a sales technique.) Note: <u>Do not reinforce negative behavior just for the sake of being supportive</u>. For example, if she breaks dates, it isn't smart to admire her spontaneous outlook on life.

3. Pick a special word or phrase to describe her. If she seems to respond (she might smile, grab your arm, or soften up when you say it), then use it consistently. Pick a word that indicates she is *smaller* and more *feminine* than you, i.e. "Bunny" or "Rosepetal." One man I dated regularly told me I was "such a little flower." He used it whenever possible, and every time he said it, it made me feel fabulous.

4. Pick her up and carry her down the street. Do <u>not</u> groan and say: *Boy, have <u>you</u> been eating a lot of potatoes!* Instead say—*You are <u>so light</u>* ! Play piggyback. Pick her up when you make love to her and cradle her in your arms. Pick her up and pin her against the wall. The point is to make her feel as if she is *smaller* than you. These tactics make you appear dominant.

5. Ask about her kids! If you want to gain her trust, she should know that you don't see them as a liability. If you *do* see them as a liability, don't go out with her! You think maybe those kids are going to go away? <u>Fat chance</u>.

6. Pay for her baby-sitter, her cat or dog-sitter, or her plane fare. Make it easy for her to say yes to you or to go away with you for a weekend. *Do not ask her to go to Mexico with you and expect her to pay her way.* In fact, did you know that the inability to pay half for weekend trips or expensive vacations often leads women to refuse these excursions because we don't want to ask, "Are you paying?" (And you thought it was because we were playing hard to get.) You also activate the influence tool of "the favor." She will feel obliged to you.

> ### You ask, you pay

Another important thing to remember about "away games." While you are thinking you are going to get lucky, she is thinking, "That means I'll have to have sex with him." The answer? In the same sentence with your suggestion to go away together tell her that of course you will both have separate rooms. She will be amazed at your willingness to accept her boundaries, your charming chivalry, and therefore might be more willing to *let* you get lucky because you are so sweet and considerate. It will be extremely difficult for her to resist you if you get separate rooms in a romantic location. This technique is successfully employed by those men who get their girlfriends to have sex by saying that they want to spend the night, but "just want to cuddle," promising that they will keep their clothes on. Right. Who do you know that's sane in the middle of the night?

7. More about you ask, you pay. Women call their girl-friends regularly to complain about men who ask them out, and then borrow money from them to pay the meal, or ask them to pay half. *"Can you believe that ?"* we say to each other as we shake our heads. You immediately fall into the loser category, and even if we are madly attracted to you, we will have a hard time not holding a grudge the next time you take us out. Your "test" of our financial independence will backfire on you. If the woman doesn't reciprocate with a meal or an offer to pay her half sometime soon into the courtship do not assume that she expects a free ride. Find out about her financial status. She may be broke.

Or, like you, *she* may have had to support *her* ex and might be testing *you.*

8. Kiss her in public. Most women enjoy this immensely. Some are uncomfortable, and you'll find out soon enough, but try it anyway. Don't ask her if you can kiss her. Just do it. From a female viewpoint, it's very sexy to be kissed when we are held up against a wall, or held by the shoulders. Think about those old movies. Did Bogart timidly reach over and plant a little peck on her cheek? No, he grabbed her and kissed her no holes barred.

9. Arrange to have her see what you do at work. This is also known as the podium effect. If you have an important job, invite her to come see you lecture, or when you are at your best, playing tennis, whatever. She will look up to you, and this, of course, makes you look figuratively larger, and therefore, more dominant.

10. Send her a drink. If she accepts that's as good as saying, you can come over and spend some time with me. It's also a favor exchange. Buy her a rose when they come by selling them at your table. Don't ask her if she wants one. Of course she wants one! (Most women say no because they don't want to look greedy.)

11. Buy her cards and send them to her for no particular reason. *"Thinking of you on this first day of Spring."* You don't need to wait for a special occasion to send one. Also, commemorate the special occasions you have together by sending a card. Think romance, romance, romance. This is what women want.

12. Find out what she likes to do and do it with her. Is this simple or what? If she like theatre, you take her there. If she likes the beach, you take her there too. If there is a simple formula it's this: find out what she likes and give it to her.

13. Have opinions, but try not to make them the oppo-site of hers. The goal here is to appear to be in sync with her, as if you are on the same wavelength. Making a point out of disagreeing with her opinions is not sexy. See Chapter Six.

14. Have desires and tell her what they are. This lets her know that you are a mover and shaker, that you don't stand in one place. However, if you are going through a period of financial difficulty, do not tell her. Unfortunately, she <u>may</u> think you are unable to pull your own weight or provide for her and you don't want her feeling sorry for you. Remember that you are trying to appear dominant, and financial dominance is extremely important. The "exceptional" women probably will be supportive, while others may "trade" your temporary financial difficulties for your good looks or great personality.

If you feel the need to, it's smarter to tell her something like—you are experiencing some <u>financial shifting</u> because of the changes in the economy or market, but also tell her the intended outcome. Say, "After this *repositioning* I'll be in a much better position to be my own boss." <u>This makes you look like a man who is in charge of his fate</u>, even if fate hasn't been so hot lately.

Tell her your hopes and dreams. This makes you look accessible and open. Especially tell her that you'd like to settle down and that you are sick of running around (even if you are not sure yet.) Tell her about your future financial plans, house building fantasies, or retirement in Fiji. She will imagine going there with you. This is based on a woman's need to settle down, and wanting a man that feels the same way.

15. Clarify your position on having children or taking care of hers if she has them. Having children is extremely important to most women who are still fertile and haven't had any yet. Save yourself heartache, grief and many an argument by talking about the following issues:

ABOUT WOMEN AND KIDS—YOURS, MINE OR OURS

- If you'd like to have children, make sure that she knows it.
- If you want your own genetic line reproduced, let her know that.
- Make sure she knows if you would consider adopting.
- If you have had a vasectomy, tell her as soon as tactfully possible.
- Figure out how old she is. If she hasn't had children and is in her thirties, she's thinking about having kids. She is "exceptional" if she hasn't had children, is still fertile and doesn't want any.
- Smart women find out right away how many kids you have, and calculate what kind of responsibility they might have to take for them. If you have primary custody of your children, this is a double-edged sword. It is a disadvantage from the woman's point of view; she will become an instant mommy and they won't be her kids. (This, of course, is a big problem for most men who date single mothers.) But it is also a positive reflection on you, for it shows you are a responsible person and not likely to go running off.
- Some women will come right out and tell you how old they are, if they haven't had children and aren't planning on having any. Some women look younger than they are, or are unable to have kids. These women don't want you to leave them for a younger woman you can have babies with after they have fallen in love with you! That's the reason smart women aren't going out with younger

men. They know that your interest in them tends to be sexual and not permanent.

- If you want kids, and she is fast approaching the age where she will be less likely to conceive, consider whether or not having kids right away would be appealing to you should you get serious and settle down. Some women spring the idea of having kids on the guy right away after the wedding. I suggest that you discuss the child issue FIRST. Do not assume anything, ever. "It ain't over 'til the fat lady sings". And we're talking a <u>special kind</u> of fat guys.

CHIVALRY

Chivalry is a sign of being from a different class of men—a higher class. Remember that high status equals high mating desirability. Women consider chivalrous behavior to be highly attractive. Good manners will make you stand apart from other men in her mind, and they can certainly make a difference in getting a second date. These behaviors are potent deal makers or breakers. Learn them and get smart.

Chivalrous Behavior That Women Respond To:

1. **Standing up** when a lady enters the room.
2. **Holding a woman's arm** as she crosses the street, or holding her elbow as she walks over precarious footing. (We know we can do it ourselves; it just feels good.)
3. **Walking on the outside** of the sidewalk (In the old days, it protected us from water splashing from carriages in the street.) If you cross to the other side of the street, putting you on the inside again, subtly switch positions. Just switch arms, stepping behind her in a smooth motion.

4. **Holding a woman's chair** for her.

5. **Lighting a woman's cigarette.**

6. **Opening the car door** for her. Say to her, "Let me get your door." Many women feel silly waiting while the man runs around the outside of the car, and most will get out on their own. However, if she is dressed formally, she will be putting on her formal manners, and will appreciate your honoring this old custom. When you return to the car, always unlock her door first. Never get in first and make her stand and wait for you to open the door from the inside. If you are going to her car, take her keys from her and unlock the car door for her. Offer to drive even if it's her car.

7. **Waiting to make sure that her car starts** before you drive off— a must for safety reasons as well! Say to her, "I'll wait to make sure that you get to your car safely."

8. **Call her to see that she gets home safely** if she has to drive a long way, or fly across the country.

9. **Ordering from the menu** for both of you. First, ask her what she will have. Then, tell the waiter, "She'll have the fish and I'll have a steak." When the waiter asks if she wants soup or salad, look at her, indicating that she should answer. After she does, go back to ordering. She'll probably chime in.

10. **Helping a woman out of a car.** Take her hand or her elbow.

11. **Paying the bill.** If she offers to pay, you thank her and refuse. Sometimes a woman will tuck her part of the bill into your pocket. Don't talk about it, just accept.

12. **Opening doors and standing aside** so she can go into elevators, restaurants, and stores first.

13. **"Seeing her to her door."** A woman who doesn't want you to kiss her, or wants to avoid asking you in will probably make a definite move to get out of the car first. Watch her body language. She will hold on to the handle of the door as she says good-bye to you and/or lean away from you. If she lingers, that is the signal that she wants to get closer to you. Wait for her to ask you in. Or, touch her hair, hold her hands, and just talk. If she looks at you quietly and smiles, you could try to kiss her. But make sure the other non-verbal signals are already in place. See Chapter Seven.

14. **Calling the following day** to say that you had a good time; keep it short and sweet. Some men believe that sending a full bouquet of flowers after the first date is acceptable behavior. There is nothing wrong with this; it is accepted in the South where well-bred men act in a chivalrous manner consistently. However, in other parts of the country, where giving flowers is less common, a full bouquet often smacks of being "overly eager." If you feel like sending flowers, send one flower instead—make her wait for more. Create anticipation.

15. **Bringing a single flower** to her door on the first date.

16. **Picking her up at her house.** Make the extra effort to drive. These days, women will want to meet you at a neutral location for at least the first date. Although we expect to drive to meet you, this doesn't mean that you should allow it. Set yourself apart from the herd and make that extra effort. This gesture also triggers the unconscious "favor" influence technique.

What do you do if, while attempting any of these behaviors, your date looks at you with murder in her eye and says nastily, "I can order for myself, thank you!" Short of getting the hell out of there and fast, you've got a woman on your hands who, because of some incidents in her past, is protecting herself. If you are attracted to her, let her do it. It does not necessarily mean she's a rabid feminist. Try using chivalry subtly and tell her that you enjoy doing these little things for her. See if she softens her position. Also remember that on the first few dates, she will be testing you, watching how you treat her. She may not allow you to act in a chivalrous way because it makes her feel vulnerable, and in the beginning some women feel they need to maintain a sense of control. After she feels safer, she will probably soften up. If she continues to act vigilant and criticizes your efforts to be kind—beware! She may never allow you to get close.

Chivalrous behavior is not only appreciated by "older" women; females in their twenties appreciate it as well so don't worry that you will offend her. More than likely, if she is younger, she will not be used to good manners, for they are being taught less and less. She may giggle, but she will appreciate your effort.

Professional athletes try to analyze game failures so they can repeat the plays that worked and avoid the ones that didn't. The same strategy works with women. Try the techniques in this chapter several times before discarding them. Try them different ways, on different days, with different women. Consider the fly which tries to get out of the room, but stupidly bangs itself against the glass time and again. The fly is not bright enough to think up another way to get out. You are.

If you think these techniques won't work, then create your own that do. I don't pretend to have all the answers. However, the techniques in this chapter are universally accepted to be extremely powerful. They are taught in the boardrooms of major corporations all over the United States. My job is to offer you the best advice available from the psychological theories of influence, mating and sexuality; your job is to choose to make yourself happy. Do what works. Don't be a depressed fly with no dates.

"...It is not the critic that counts, not the man who points out how the strong man stumbled or where the doer of deeds could have done better. The credit belongs to the man who is actually in the arena: whose face is marred by dust and sweat and blood; who strives valiantly, who knows the great enthusiasms, the great devotions, and spends himself in a worthy cause; who at the worst, if he fails, at least he fails while daring bravely so that his place shall never be with those cold and timid souls who know neither victory or defeat." —T. Roosevelt

They had been engaged only a few weeks, but a little coolness had arisen between them.

"There is nothing that makes me so angry," she cried, with tears of rage in her blue eyes, "as to have anyone contradict me. I just simply hate to be contradicted by anyone."

"Well," he said in a conciliatory tone, "I won't do it any more."

"I don't believe you love me much anyway," she asserted.

"I don't," he readily admitted.

"You are a perfectly hateful thing, so you are!"

"I know it."

"You are trying to tease me, aren't you?"

"Yes."

She was silent a short time, then said,

"Well, I certainly do despise a man who is weak enough to let a woman dictate to him. A man ought to have a mind of his own."

How To 6 Talk To A Woman

After a date, she calls up her friends and says, "He's great, but he doesn't know how to talk." *As women, we all know exactly what that means.* As men, it's hard to make it to first base unless you master this extremely important skill. Most men are able to carry on business conversations, and some men can carry on small talk, but very few are good at expressing their emotions. Sharing feelings is extremely important to a woman, and it's something that doesn't come easily for most men. Why should it? You weren't socialized to express your feelings. Women want you to talk because it comes naturally to <u>them</u>, because they learned to fight verbally instead of physically. I realize that women need to learn to back off in this area, but this book is written for you.

You don't have to play by her rules, in fact, it's vital that you don't if you want to maintain your power in the relationship, but you absolutely *do* need to:

1. Learn to how to approach women and open with small talk.

2. Find out what she's like so you can know whether you want go out with her.

3. Lead the conversation into areas that will make it easy for you to comfortably ask her out.

4. Express feelings you have about her.

Here is a formula for a great approach. This works when you are rusty, have never had much luck, never seem to know what to say, or you feel like a petrified toad.

1. Stand near her and <u>mirror</u> her body language. This means to match what she is doing in a subtle way (see Chapter Seven on mirroring.)

2. Let a few minutes elapse, and take in the environment. If you're at a bar, order a drink; if you're at a buffet table, linger in the same area and graze. This is a good time to breathe and send yourself positive self-talk (I think I can I think I can). If you are really nervous, do what public speakers do. Imagine her naked! That's the ticket. . . You can also use any of the anxiety reducing techniques in Chapter Twelve.

3. Now, begin to talk using this formula:

Point 1 Say something to her about what is going on in your immediate environment. *"Boy, the cheese dip is great tonight."*

Point 2 Say something personal about yourself regarding that cue; it endears you to us, and makes you look open. *"I really like the swiss cheese myself."*

Point 3 Ask an open-ended question—use words like: what, how, I wonder, why, when. "What kind of cheese do you think this dip is made from?"

Here is a "Triangle" Approach

Point 1) "Boy, the band is playing some really strange numbers."

Point 2) "I really prefer Latin, myself. I feel a little out of place."

Point 3) "<u>What</u> kind of music is the band playing, anyway, can you figure out what this is?" Or <u>when</u> do you think they'll play something good? Or <u>I wonder</u> why there aren't many people here? Or <u>what</u> do you think?

- Remember to pause between the points. She doesn't like being peppered with questions.
- How, what, and why are good words that allow her to give an answer that isn't just yes or no.

Consider: "Do you like the cheese dip?"

"No" — a failed maneuver.

Practice this three point formula whenever you have down time. Say that you're in an elevator. Ask yourself how you would start a casual conversation with someone there.

Point 1) "What's the line like in the lunch room?"

Point 2) "I'm thinking that maybe I'll go across the street to that hamburger place today."

Point 3) "Would you like to go with me instead of standing in that line?"

OTHER APPROACHES THAT WORK:

- "Hi Jane. . . .Oh, I'm sorry, you looked like Jane, well, hello anyway, I'm Jon," and other variations of, "You look just like Jane, only better."
- "Do you come here OFTEN? (Said in a way to exaggerate this overused phrase, then you smirk.)
- "Well, hi there, fancy meeting you over the cole-slaw. . . . Did you try the carrots? They're spectacular!" (Said in an amusing tone.)

- Don't forget the humble approach used by many with great success. It's my personal favorite. "Hi, My name is Tom, I just couldn't leave here tonight without meeting you." No kidding, this works. It's direct and to the point.

- Another very effective way to break the ice is to start with where you are. If you're nervous, you can say, "You know, I've never been very good at introducing myself to pretty women, and I wish I knew just the right thing to say at moments like this, but I'd really like to meet you. . . . I'm Tom," then smile and let her talk. This is an ingenious and comfortable way to be yourself. She sees your human, vulnerable side and this will attract her. The only thing you need to remember is to keep your vocal tone level and strong and your eye contact direct.

Using What She's Doing to Approach

Notice what she's doing. If she's reading an interesting magazine you say, "Are you reading about the game?" or any other current event. If she's buying a latte, you say: "Aren't the lattes good here?" Then you go on to the second point of the conversational triangle. . . "I usually get vanilla in mine." . . Then to the third point, "Have you ever had almond?"

Using Compliments to Meet Her

Go very lightly. Try to find something she is wearing or carrying to comment on. If she is wearing an interesting pin, hat or has an artistic looking purse, you start there. Laptops, class rings, and just about anything can work for you. "That's an unusual bracelet, where did you get it?" Continue with point number two, "Oh, it's from France, eh? Did you get it there? I went to Paris last year." Do not comment directly on her fabulous figure, or legs. This is too personal and makes her feel like a porkchop. The most you can get away with, if you're really smooth and natural, is complimenting her on her beautiful hair or striking eyes if she has them.

If you want to go out with her, ask her for her number; do not give her your business card and casually ask her to call you sometime. She is left thinking, what is this, business or pleasure? Or she feels irritated at your indirect behavior, "Why didn't he just ask me for my number?" Although *you* may be trying to avoid rejection, *she* hasn't a clue about whether you like her or not—she can't read your mind! And she might just think you are not interested. In addition, putting the woman in the position to call you is not considered polite behavior by women who were socialized to expect the man to call. It gives YOU with the upper hand. Yes, *you* have to do the work to get her attention. If she wants to be careful about giving out her home number, but really likes you, she will give you her work number.

If you are feeling bold, ask her straight out for a more romantic activity.

What a sexy thing for a man to come right out and do! The big selling point to the direct approach is that you immediately know whether she's interested in you and you avoid a lot of wasted time fantasizing about her. If she agrees, she's almost always interested. If she's not interested, she will waffle or act indecisive. This gives you important evidence. It is now up to you to decide whether she's worth trying to fight for. Consider the evidence, then plan further strategies. If she refuses a Friday date, you can always counter with lunch on Thursday. If she refuses Thursday, you say in a humorous voice, "How about coffee Wednesday after work?" It's a well-known fact in sales psychology that it's hard to say no to a person three times. This foot-in-the-door approach will give you more time to persuade her to go out on a real date with her. If you have started with the bigger request, it will be hard for her to refuse a third, less romantic one, the simple cup of coffee. The casual coffee approach works well when you've known each other through business, or if you've just met. So, you can go with the big request, a real date, or you can ask for the coffee date first. How much time can <u>you</u> afford to waste?

> **Everyday above ground is a good day**

OTHER WAYS TO ASK HER OUT

<u>First, steer the conversation around to an activity that you discover she likes.</u> It took me awhile before I figured this maneuver out. It's very clever. A guy would ask me if I wanted to try out a new dive spot and I was always looking for a scuba buddy. Then I realized that there was more going on than just going diving together. Because we're sexual animals—there's ALWAYS something going on besides the fact that he "needs a dive partner." You can bet your bulldog that if a woman says she's looking for a tennis partner— she's coming on to you.

She does not JUST WANT A TENNIS PARTNER.

In the same vein, you can get your foot in the door by doing something together that you both have in common and she's more likely to find you attractive, because an experience she likes has been linked with you. You immediately take on the positive aspects of the food, or the sport, or the environment that she likes. The other night, a friend took me to the river for dinner. He immediately attained good guy status because water, an element that I love, was connected with being with him.

So, you have discussed French food, and she likes it. You ask her out this way. "Say, I heard there's a new French restaurant that's opening on Lombard; why don't you give me your number and we'll go sometime." Get it? Maybe WE should go, not "Would you like to go out with me to this new French restaurant?" Using <u>we</u> takes the pressure off.

Let's say you are at a dance and you find out that she likes swing dancing; you're good at it, and you start talking with her about the places she's been to dance. Then you say that there's a new place to dance around the corner and suggest ". . .getting some people together to go there. Why don't you give me your number and I'll call everyone. . ." Other ways to do it: (after a discussion about her work), "I really want to find out more about _____, do you mind if I call you sometime to pick your brain? Or she says that she's always wanted to get into kayaking after she finds out that you are a kayaker, (this indicates a <u>definite</u> possibility that she wants you to ask her out). So you merely say, "Well, I'm going out next weekend, you want to come along?"

<u>Why</u> **is a really good word that can keep the conversation going.** "<u>Why</u> did you decide to go into nursing I wonder?". . ." <u>Why</u> do you suppose that the weather has been so strange?"

GENERAL RULES

First: Get her talking, figure out what you have in common and tell her about it.

Second: She wants to know if you are interested in her or not. Please, gentlemen. . . .

If you like her, make your intentions known.

HOW WOMEN TEST YOU DURING CONVERSATION

<u>Point out what you have in common, not how you are different.</u> The goal is to appear to be in sync with her—as if you are on the same wave length. Making a point out of your differences or dislike of her hobbies is not sexy. In addition, use the same words she does when you are talking. Listen to her, then repeat her opinions in a different form.

> **Right:** She says she likes the women's movement because it has helped stop sexism. You say, "Yeah, the movement really went a long way to help the legal system change its <u>sexist</u> position. What do you think about male custody rights?" (Here, you use one of HER words, <u>sexism</u>, to get her to continue talking so you'll find out more about just HOW radical she is.)
>
> **Wrong:** "Feminists? What a joke. Women have been taking advantage of men for centuries, and now we have to give them our jobs too?" (Now she thinks you are out to slam her and she's ready to punch you out. You are no longer the good guy; you are just another "sexist" to her. You don't need to be fighting with her, you need to be making LOVE to her, remember?)

<u>Know how women react to men who talk TOO much about their feelings.</u> These are men who have a poor sense of what are called "boundaries." A personal boundary means the imaginary line where your business stops and her business starts. Men with poor boundaries try to get women to fill up their emptiness. They throw themselves at the woman by constantly calling her, buying her gifts and expensive dinners, or agreeing with all her ideas. And they don't fight back when she criticizes or complains unfairly.

HOW SHE SCREENS YOU

A woman tests you in specific ways when she begins talking to you. She doesn't tell you about them, but if you don't pass her screening, you might not get any farther. What she initially wants to know:

1. Are you married or separated? Most importantly: How long have you physically been away from your wife? (The smart woman wants to avoid being the first relationship after the divorce, "rebounds" rarely work out.) Tell her what she wants to know. For example, "I've been physically separated for six months."

2. Your occupation. She wants to know generally how financially secure you are. The tangible objects you own, a house, a boat, a great car are clues that tell her about your financial status. Tactfully let her know all of the important information. Exaggerated boasts about your financial status will come out eventually. You don't have to flash your Rolex at her, but short of offering tax statements, she wants to know what your financial situation is and she doesn't want her time wasted with a man who is not of her financial preference. Relax, most women just want to know that you make about as much money as they do. Don't be fooled by stories that you will look ostentatious by telling the truth. If you are the president of a law firm, say so. However, if you do "consulting," she will want to know a little more about it.

Does this whole money thing offend you? Well, imagine what it's like to be judged in the first ten seconds on your looks, which is what women have to put with; at least with the money issue you can get in a few seconds of conversation.

3. If you have children and if you want any more.

4. What hobbies and activities you like. Athletic women want to know your level of activity. Educated women want to know about your schooling and what social circles you move in. Nerdettes want to know what programs you've worked on.

<u>**Complimenting her is extremely important.**</u> Say: "You make that dress look beautiful." Rather than "the <u>dress</u> makes you look good." When she is talking a lot, you compliment her observations, "You sound like you've been studying psychology, <u>when</u> did you learn all that?" Or, "There's nothing more beautiful than a smart woman."

<u>**Do detective work.**</u> Discover what she believes no one appreciates about her personality—figure out what her hidden, less than obvious strengths are. Let her know that you do appreciate her for them. For example, admire how hard she tries, how wonderful it is that she is so emotional (even if it scares the hell out of you); praise her artistic ability. If she has a beautiful figure, <u>you</u> talk about how smart she is. If she has a Ph.D., compliment her beauty. Learn the obvious, then compliment her on those hidden talents. She's *used* to hearing about her beautiful legs if she has them—so you will talk about her artistic ability. Tell her what you admire about her. It is important to tell her things that others probably haven't. (You zig when they zag.) If she's the independent type, tell her you appreciate her softness and vulnerability (that's what she's protecting.) If she appears delicate or fragile, tell her you like her strength in work or other areas which you know she enjoys.

HOW TO DEAL WITH IT WHEN "SHE WANTS TO TALK"

First of all, dogs bark, bugs crawl, and woman like to talk—a LOT. Get used to it. And when the relationship heats up, she's going to want to have these TALKS. Instead of rolling your eyes, learn to like these periods. HOW? Well, maybe in the same way I started liking basketball. My guy was totally into it, and in order to be with him, we went to a lot of games. I could fight it and be alone, or I could go with it.

To a woman, having a nice talk is one of the most important things she does with her man. The problem is that she likes to find fault when things aren't going well. <u>This is because she really wants you to "take care of her" and make her feel better</u> (again, it is unconscious protection.) A man's first impulse may be to try to fix the misunderstanding, but she just wants you to LISTEN. She wants to be appreciated. Perhaps she doesn't feel like she's getting what she wants, or maybe she feels lonely. She wants more closeness and warm fuzzies.

Perhaps she is the kind of woman who never feels like she is getting enough no matter what you've done for her. Even if this is true it doesn't help to tell her this. If you love her, you must accept that this is her weakness, not find fault with her. I'm talking about unconditional regard. I'm talking about going the extra yard and being the bigger man.

WHAT TO DO WHEN SHE STARTS TO COMPLAIN

1. <u>Listen completely to what she has to say</u>. Then decide for yourself if she has something up her nose, or a legitimate gripe. Unfortunately, her gripes will usually have something to do with you.

2. <u>Legitimate gripes</u>. This requires some honesty on your part about your less than cool qualities. If you don't have a clue about what your weaknesses are, ask yourself if you've heard this complaint before from other girlfriends, business associates or even your mother! If her complaints could possibly be accurate, tell her that she has a good point, thank her for the feedback (actually say this phrase, it works) and then, tell her that you want to think about it for awhile.

3. <u>Do not grovel at her feet</u> apologizing profusely about how you are just a pile of dirt and oh she is so right! (Even if she <u>is</u> right, she doesn't have to <u>know</u> about it all the time.) This gives her undue influence over you and makes you look more and more like a doormat.

4. <u>Legitimate gripes that you've heard before.</u> After you've figured out that you've heard this complaint twenty times before and you have already talked about it several times, decide whether you need to discuss it again. Ask her what she wants that she feels she isn't getting and why is she continuing to talk about it? (Try to use a civil tone and fight your animal instinct to club her.) Listen carefully and make sure you understand what the complaint is about. <u>Often, women just need to say what they feel and it has very little to do with what you have or haven't done.</u>

5. <u>Use active listening</u>. Repeat to her what you think she said. For example, after she stops talking, ask her if she is through. Then say, "So what you're telling me is that ____," repeating to her what you think she's said, and asking for clarification. For example: "So you're saying that you don't think I spend enough time with you, is that right?" When she agrees that yes, you have heard her correctly, tell her you need some time to try to give her what she wants, adding that you hope that's OK with her. She'll find it hard to disagree. Then change the subject and genuinely try to give her what she wants.

VERBAL PROCESSING AND/OR GENERAL MOODINESS

1. <u>"Verbal processing" by a woman means that she is thinking out loud.</u> Women often figure out their problems while they are talking about them. Sometimes they will just get moody and start meandering around about some vague subject or other. Eventually they may come to some sort of statement or question at the end of this monologue that they toss out for your response. It's best not to interrupt this speech while it is under way. Know that a great deal of this kind of monologue may just be "emotional venting", and, as such should not be taken completely seriously. This female behavior is sort of like what men do during the Super Bowl. Do not, however, let her know that <u>you know</u> she is just venting. This may enrage her, and she could accuse you of "not really listening" or phrases to that effect. (Try to imagine how you would feel if we turned off the Super Bowl and disregarded your protestations!) As you get to know her better, you'll be able to read her moods and adjust your responses accordingly. To help clarify these "verbal processing sessions" consider this:

2. If her topic isn't you, what works really well is to ask her, "Do you want some feedback, or do you just need me to listen?" This will avoid an accusal that you are "trying to tell her what to do."

DO NOT TRY TO FIX HER —
THIS WILL NOT WORK

Men have this need to try to help out and that is natural, but most women don't know this and they will accuse you of trying to control them. And sometimes you ARE trying to do just that! (Probably so that they'll shut up—right?) Remember, acting like you have all the answers and telling her that she should listen to you is acting like a <u>jerk</u>, but having your own opinions about what she is discussing without implying that she should agree is being <u>balanced</u>. Heh.

3. If her topic is you, listen and go through the steps I mentioned above. Do not skip steps and immediately assume her words are not to be taken seriously, investigate first. You could have some habit that really drives her nuts or hurts her, and she could actually leave you because of it! It would be a serious mistake to disregard her complaints as idle bitchiness.

Rule: A woman will rarely complain about her unhappiness with the relationship unless you are somehow contributing to the problem.

You need to "weed the yard on <u>your</u> side of the fence." Always consider how YOU are contributing to the problems in your relationship first. Change what YOU can change, it is up to her to handle with her own issues. If you can't work together to find solutions, <u>get couples counseling</u>. Remember that attempting to give her what she wants does not make you a doormat, as long as what she asks for is not unreasonable. What's unreasonable? Here is a list of what women don't have a right to ask of you, if they want to keep you around—unless you enjoy being a doormat!

A LIST OF UNREASONABLE DEMANDS

1. To talk to her <u>constantly</u> about your feelings. She thinks that you should react to the world the way she does? She is a female, you are a male. Try to remember this.

2. To immediately talk to her when you come home from work when you are exhausted, want to turn on some TV and unwind. Especially if she's been sitting around all day waiting for you to come home. She thinks that on top of being tired you should turn yourself inside out to please her? Get a grip, girl!

3. To have a child with her because you are a couple and <u>she</u> wants to have one. It is perfectly possible for you to love

her AND not want to have babies. If you do want to have one, it should be because you want to share bringing up a child, and are prepared to give that child all the attention it needs, not to keep her from leaving you. If all she wants is a baby maker, move on.

Rule: Children should not form the glue that keeps you together. The relationship is the foundation upon which the child grows! An unstable foundation will create an unstable child.

---

4. To have to learn her household habits and do things the way she wants them done. If she is messy, does that mean you should be? If she compulsively cleans lint out of the dryer, does that mean you don't care about her if you don't? Learn to live with your differences. Learn to barter or exchange tasks. She will not leave you because of your household habits. But watch out! Continuous superficial struggles are symptoms of deeper problems in the relationship.

5. To put aside your "guy" activities in order to please her. This is a needy, selfish position. You should both have other friends and outside activities and spend time away from each other doing your own thing.

6. To listen to her feelings about other men she is dating. This is guaranteed to put you in the friend category.

"Friend" is another word for "NO SEX"

STOPPING HER COMPLAINTS

Once you have decided that she is making unreasonable remands, that her topic is not serious or that she's not talking in a way that makes much sense to you (translate this to mean she is lonely and she needs attention), you have several unique and fun options. You don't want her to criticize your lack of response. So, you have to interrupt this feedback loop and let her know that you aren't going to take this lying down (like a doormat!)

1. First interrupt the pattern. Immediately change body positions if you can, or stop doing what you are doing and do something different. Try hugging her or kissing her. Ask, "Do you need a hug?" or just give her one while still allowing her to complain. Do not attempt to combat her words. Counter with action, that is your male strength. If she allows you to hug her and kiss her, she may wind down her argument and show her softer side. Being affectionate works.

> *Note: Do not kiss and hug her if she is criticizing you! This will condition the tantrum. This means that if you reward her (the hug) when she's doing something you don't like, she will do it even more. Whenever you reward a behavior, it will get stronger. Only use physical affection when she is talking about generalized relationship problems of a less serious note.*

- If you are in the car (a favorite time for her to have your full attention and keep you captive when she starts complaining), you stop at a filling station and disappear to go to the john. This gives her time to cool down and interrupts her monologue. Or, you stop for a soda or take a side road and start talking about the beautiful trees. Anything to change the direction of the conversation.

- If you are at home, leave the room you are in and go into another room. Begin doing something else. If she complains that you are not listening, say to her, "I'll make a deal with you. I'll listen to you if you will just simply tell me what you want that you're not getting, and stop talking to me in that tone of voice." Then listen. If she continues in the same tone, or interrupts you, leave.

- If you are in front of others when she starts in, say excuse me to the others and leave. When she catches up with you, tell her in no uncertain terms **not to talk to you like that**. Tell her if she does it again, you will walk away again.

2. Use strong language. You might tell her calmly that she's acting like a BITCH and to QUIT IT. Talkative women respond remarkably well to blunt statements like this. (In fact, women sometimes get aroused by safe verbal aggression. Words like "bitch" and "baby" when used in a playful tone are actually sexy to certain "exceptional" women.)

3. Leave. If she escalates, and gets upset at any of your interrupt-the-pattern behaviors, excuse yourself, tell her you are going for a walk, going to the john, going home (or worse, *going to take her home*). Tell her that you'll come back when she's ready to stop being bitchy.

- In animal language you have established that you aren't going to let her dominate you and that if she chooses to fight you are ready to fight back. She will respect you when you draw the line and let her know that she can't get away with mistreating you.

ASSERTIVE VERBAL BEHAVIOR

Women watch you to see how assertive you are. They are looking for decisive behavior. Wishy-washy decisions are a turn-off. Here are some examples of assertive and non-assertive dialogues.

Assertive	Passive
1. To the waiter: "We want a booth please—we're willing to wait."	1. As you are following the waiter your girlfriend says: "Could we get a booth?"
2. She says her meat is underdone. You call the waiter and tell him to cook it more.	2. She says her meat is underdone. You say, "What do you want to do about it?" She says, "I don't know." Later, she says to you, "We should have sent it back." She wanted <u>you</u> to send it back.
3. At a movie, she can't see over the head of the person in front of her. You immediately switch places with her, or tell her you'll move to the better seats. You select the new seats, after making sure she likes them.	3. You say, "Oh, you'll be OK after the movie starts," (a jerk response) or "There probably aren't any other good seats," (a doormat response). Then, you make no move to help the situation out.
4. She says her lawn mower is broken. You set a time and come over to fix it. Remember, women like men who do physical, practical things for them. (but make sure she isn't just getting you to help her and avoiding romance, that is doormatdom.)	4. She says her lawnmower is broken. Although you can fix it, you don't want to presume she can't take care of herself. You say, "Oh, too bad," or you suggest a place where she can take it. <u>Why do you think women even bring these things up to begin with?</u> Yes, we do need and appreciate help from men.

Assertive	Passive
5. A clerk ignores you. You say, "May I have some service here?"	5. A clerk ignores you. You wait patiently.
6. You call your girlfriend. You immediately say, "Hi, Judy, great to hear your voice. Let's go out Friday, whatdaya say?"	6. You call your girlfriend to talk. You say, "Oh, hi Susan. It's Jeff. I was wondering if…you're probably busy or have a date, but if you're not, I'd like to take you out sometime, if that's OK with you." Or you say, "What are you doing Friday night?" (We know you're going to ask us out, so we'll counter with, "Nothing, why?") This is very weak behavior.
7. "Let's go to the aquarium, would you like that?"	7. You: "So, where do you want to go?"
	Her: "Um, I don't know." (She's trying to get you to decide; she likes this better.)

Rule for Number 7: You take the assertive position by deciding what to do and where to go on your dates. If she says she really wants to go see a movie or an opening, you agree. But, on the next date, you decide and stick to it.

A General Rule for Assertive Speech

Have opinions and state them. Try not to disagree with her opinions; it's important that you both appear to be on the same wave length. Instead, have additional statements and ideas about her position. So, if she loves opera and you hate it, you don't have to say so. Instead, you say, "It must take a lot of work to learn how to sing that well."

An assertive man is a doer, a mover, a decider. If she has any sort of personal strength, she's been deciding, suggesting, pushing, prodding, trying to get men to be more gutsy for years. She will admire, be attracted to and relieved by your assertiveness. She will probably let you lead as much as you like, as long as you remember to be emotionally supportive.

ON ATTITUDE

Here is a thought that may help you focus less on her needs and more on your own:

It does not matter if I am good enough for HER
But if SHE is good enough for ME!

If she doesn't have to work to keep your interest sometime in the relationship, it will be one-sided. She'll get bored with you and move on. I can't stress this enough. **You must value yourself.** The way to do this is to find out whether or not SHE appreciates YOU. If she doesn't, you should leave! So, do not throw yourself at her.

You have a right to walk the face of the earth. Start noticing how you apologize for yourself in your attitude and your speech. If you feel that you are somewhere lower than a slug in a latté, we should talk. Remember that even John Wayne wore lifts in his shoes. And walking tall is an acquired skill. If you practiced confident conversation as much as you watched TV or netsurfed, you'd get dates. Just DO it!

Because you didn't grow up knowing how to express your feelings, you are probably less talkative than she is, and you are probably not used to sharing with someone when you are feeling low. Practice communicating EVERY DAY. Notice when you are upset about something. This is prime time to talk about it. That's what she does. DON'T stuff it. DON'T tell yourself it doesn't matter. It DOES matter to you, and you are certainly not going to get what you want by hoping she will read your mind. (Although, women do have an uncanny way of figuring out what it is that you want and accusing you of it.) Practice standing up for yourself in all circumstances. The jerk knows how to do this and she respects him for it.

You might be interested to know that when my male clients start becoming assertive at work, they start dating. They get promotions and they change jobs. A dating problem is just one of the symptoms of lowered self-esteem. Other symptoms include money problems, work problems and family problems. If you can't communicate with women, chances are your communication skills with others could be improved as well.

If you don't learn some verbal skills, women will be forever pulling on you, peppering you with questions about what you are thinking, feeling, and asking, "Is something bothering you?"

You have the sympathy of every other male in America.

"He that has
eyes to see and
ears to hear may
convince himself
that no mortal
can keep a
secret. If his lips
are silent, he
chatters with his
finger tips;
betrayal oozes
out of him at
every pore."

—*Freud*

Reading Her Body Language 7

The non-verbal information that a woman unconsciously sends through her various gestures and body positions is extremely helpful when you are trying to figure out how she feels about you. This physical behavior is the best indicator of when to approach a woman, for, as you know, her spoken messages can be misleading. Society inhibits our verbal expression; it's not OK to be direct. As men you know it's much easier to say "I'll call you," when you don't plan on doing it at all. Non-verbal signs of emotion are less monitored by the conscious brain, so it's easier to get a clearer message, once you understand the signals. Open body language shows others on an instinctual level that you are harmless, that they can come closer; hostile body language can put an abrupt halt to romantic feelings.

Actions such as adjusting clothing, protruding the chest, giving sideways glances, touching the hair, face, or cheek are the result of the stress of courtship as sexual energy begins to rise. Female body movements send unconscious messages that a man's presence has an effect. And if you learn these small nuances that are always present, if you learn the vocabulary of her gestures and watch closely as her body talks, you will find it much easier to get what you want.

"I am receptive to you," she is saying in animal language as she shows submissive gestures such as shoulder-shrugging, opened palms, head-tilting, joining her hands, grasping her neck, holding her upper arms or forearms (or any other self-clinging position), looking down, and rotating her feet inwards. If she's out on a date with you she might take a lower position than you in the car, especially if she feels romantic. Note that she doesn't say to herself, "I'll scrunch down in the seat so he'll kiss me." Her body just does it automatically.

The more she is attracted to you, the longer the periods of staring, smiling, preening, head -tossing, exaggerated laughter, vigorous hand and arm gestures. The tempo will be faster-paced as her sexual drive surfaces. If you don't show some interest in her after these kinds of cues, she may eventually look for a more receptive guy.

A woman can cut off communication from you by turning her body away, not looking at you, or staring blankly without smiling over her shoulder at you. When you approach her, watch the <u>angle</u> at which she is turning toward you. Does she keep her body turned ahead and away from you, only turning her head to carry on a discussion? This is a block; she's not attracted to you right now, but maybe it will change. Watch for a while and notice if she opens up and turns toward you as the conversation unfolds.

Look at the three diagrams on the following page to see the progressive level of interest as shown by the body angle she takes toward you.

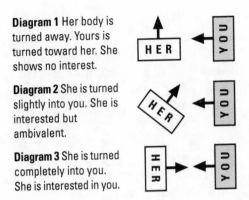

Diagram 1 Her body is turned away. Yours is turned toward her. She shows no interest.

Diagram 2 She is turned slightly into you. She is interested but ambivalent.

Diagram 3 She is turned completely into you. She is interested in you.

If she sees you approaching from a distance and already knows that she is not attracted to you, she might deliberately turn her back on you or walk away. She is certainly aware that she is doing this, but sometimes it <u>is</u> just coincidence for she hasn't seen you yet, so don't jump to conclusions. Try to approach from another angle and watch to see if she turns her back again.

If you are sitting next to her at a bar and she doesn't want to talk, she'll turn away from you, or continuously block you by keeping her shoulder between the two of you, or keeping her body faced straight ahead, turning her head only when she speaks. Or, you will see that the arm which is closest to you is held out between the two of you with her drink as a kind of barrier. This is an unconscious guarding signal; she's not aware that she's doing it. Or, she'll get up and change seats to make it clear that she doesn't want to communicate. Try seating yourself one seat away to begin with and watch to see if her body language opens up. You can strike up a conversation, and then move over if she turns in to you.

You should know that when a guy sits next to a woman at a bar, she immediately feels on guard. (Unless she is a barfly of course, or has had one too many.) She feels on guard because the space between bar stools is too close for her to feel comfortable right away, and just because she's at a bar doesn't mean she's easy, or wants to get picked up. Sure, she's aware that it is a sexual environment, and that's why she's even more on her guard. Keep a social distance of <u>three to eight feet</u> in these kinds of places to begin with. After you strike up a conversation with her, you can move closer. If she doesn't act friendly after a few conversation starters, <u>don't ask her why she is in there anyway if she doesn't want to talk</u>. (This has happened to my clients a lot!) Maybe she just doesn't want to talk with you! (Sorry.)

What happens if you leave a seat between you two and another guy moves in and sits there? To prevent this, lay your jacket over the vacant seat. If you are clearly talking with her, he will have to ask if the seat is taken. Say yes, and then move over. If you can't do this in time, (she's obviously pretty and other men WILL move in), quickly offer to buy her another drink to maintain contact, and/or stand and come around the other side of her to continue the conversation. Remember that when you are standing and she is sitting <u>you</u> are in the dominant position, though you may feel awkward. See the end of this chapter about assertive male body posture.

Does she ambivalently turn toward you and then away whether she is seated or standing? She's trying to make up her mind whether or not she likes you. Initially, when you get in her territory, she may drift away from you a little to check you out. This is similar to what you do after a woman walks by; looking at her body when you think she can't see you. So, a wise thing to do at this point is to get just close enough to her so that she can check you out without looking obvious. If you get too close, she can't do this, and so she'll move away to check you out. Remember, she's screening you for the way you dress to see whether you are of the same status. Initially, after she unconsciously registers your presence, if she likes what she sees, she will linger in your area until you make a verbal approach.

Watch for subtle smiles when you are near her, as well as any of the behaviors on the list below. Do not expect her to make the first verbal move. If she knows how to flirt, she will look at you in a coy fashion with her head tilted down, then she'll smile and look away, perhaps several times. Women who don't know how to flirt will appear to look at you blankly, or will dart furtive glances at you, holding their emotions under wraps, but you can tell if she's interested by watching for these additional signs of non-verbal attraction:

1. She may twist her hair around in her fingers, toss her hair, touch the back of her neck, or adjust her clothing.

2. She may turn her body toward you.

3. She may raise her eyebrows.

4. She may avert her gaze downward, especially when you get closer to her.

5. She may dangle one shoe off her foot.

6. She may get up and walk across your field of vision to do some errand like go to the phone or to the restroom— several times.

7. She may bend over near you so that you can see her body.

8. She may twist the stem of a wine glass, or absent-mindedly finger its rim.

9. She may cross and uncross her legs indicating a sexual message, or nonchalantly touch her legs or thighs.

10. She may lean over and whisper something to her girlfriend.

Some of these signals may be planned, and some of them may not be. All of them occur unconsciously when a woman is feeling attraction. Experienced flirts do several of these signals all the time, just like some men purposefully take off their coats and flex their muscles slightly to show off their chests.

The purpose of these non-verbal gestures is to get you to come to her. If she's consciously trying to attract you, you can figure out what she's doing because she appears in your sight line more than once in a half hour period, perhaps several times. How many times does this girl *really* need to go to the phone or to the powder room or talk with the waiter? You will see her everywhere you look. If you are dancing in a certain part of the dance floor, there she is. If you are at the buffet table, surprise! She's there too. Is this random coincidence? I think not! She's trying to make it easy for you to meet her. It's done constantly by women. And if you don't pick up on these cues, if you assume that these "coincidences" are just chance, and don't take action, you could miss out on a lot of great women. So don't <u>expect</u> her to smile when she likes you; just be glad that she did. And if you aren't noticing these signals, but you still are attracted to her, you need to remind yourself:

It doesn't matter whether she is attracted to me, but whether I am attracted to her

---

Do not expect her to come up and talk with you!

After she's sent a number of non-verbal signals, she figures that you will get the clue. Of course, what women don't understand is that you guys don't usually GET clues. That's why I wrote this book.

Look at the girl you want to attract.

Eye contact is important and sexy. Direct, long-held gazes usually happen unconsciously at more advanced stages in a relationship, but can be used at an earlier stage to intentionally send the message that you are interested in her. It is very smart to attempt eye contact from a distance at first when you spot a woman you like. It will be easier for her to smile back at you. If you are closer, it is more difficult and intimate for you both to smile at each other. Do it anyway! I ask my clients to practice and hold a three-second smile with those they are interested in attracting. I am not talking about a grinning, toothy smile; I am suggesting a quiet, confident, direct glaze. It is very sexy when a man looks at a woman and holds her gaze. You can also try a simple nod signaling, "I see you and I am interested." It sure beats thinking "Oh, my Gawd, she's the most beautiful thing in the world and I don't deserve her!" while you avoid looking directly at her. Furtive, darting glances from men are not attractive. The direct gaze is.

Try to hold a confident, shoulders back, head up body posture as well. Men who hunch over don't send a strong impression. Be sure to keep your body a little above her. This simulates dominance and power and is sexually attractive. Tall, slender men often hunch over and it looks weak and mousy. If you are shorter, remember to stand tall.

Eye contact psychologically reduces the distance between people, and signals that the lines of communication are open. When two people approach each other, eye contact decreases as they get closer. This psychologically *increases* the physical distance, and adds a safety factor. So don't worry if she looks away as you make your move. Remember that old, popular song—"Millions of people go by, but they all disappear from view—cause I only have eyes for you"? **Always remember to smile at the woman you are interested in.** Smile regularly and you will give pleasure to any person you are around.

Most women tend to look down and from under their hair, or from the side when they flirt, rarely looking right at you. But assertive women do look directly at men, which sometimes puts men off. In animal language, these women are holding their ground with you. If this appeals to you, match her by holding her gaze. If she begins to become attracted to you, her body position may soften and she will probably start looking sideways, or down and up, unconsciously indicating submission. Notice that I told you to **match** her gaze. This brings us to an important body language tool called **mirroring**.

MIRRORING BODY RHYTHMS

Partners who are attracted to each other naturally "mirror" one another, dancing to each other's rhythms. Couples who have been together for long periods of time often walk and talk at the same rate. If you want to show that you are on the same wave length, mirroring is extremely important to practice. For example, the content of a discussion between a therapist and patient tends to be positive when the body postures of each are mirror-imaged and not as positive when their bodies aren't moving in sync. Similar body positioning happens naturally among friends, colleagues, and people we have been close to for any length of time. These synchronized patterns show that we are "open" to one another.

How To Do It

As you are facing her, watch what she is doing. If she is playing with her fork, you should play with something else on the table. It's OK to play with your fork too, but don't do it obviously and wait a few beats before you begin. Is she leaning over to one side? You lean that way too. That is, as you look at her, if she is leaning to HER left, you will lean to YOUR right. She leans forward, you wait a few beats, then you lean forward. Is she tapping her foot? You tap your fingers on the table to the same beat. I'm not implying "Simon says" mirroring, and doing the same thing that she is doing, but repeating the same kind of movements as if you were looking in a mirror, which is where the term comes from.

OTHER FORMS OF MATCHING

Pace Her Vocal Speed

If she talks rapidly, you should talk rapidly; if she speaks slowly you do the same.

Pace Her Vocal Inflection

Her: "Oh **REALLY**, why?" (Louder on the **REALLY**.)

You: "Well, **BECAUSE** I want to." (Louder on because.)

Her: "I **LIKE YOU**." (stress on the two end words)

You: "So **DO I**." (identical stress as mirror)

If her voice goes up on the end, so should yours. Pace the volume as well. If it starts loud, then tapers off, yours should do the same.

Match Her Facial Expressions

If she looks bored, you look bored; if she frowns, you frown. Have you ever wondered why you don't like it when someone says, "Smile!"? It's because they have pointed out that it's not OK for you to be feeling the way you do. Women particularly hate having someone say that because smiling usually has been drilled into them; and, though it's true that smiling is more attractive, when we truly feel down, we don't like some stranger coming up to us and pointing out our gloom. How does this work with mirroring? Well, if you see a girl who looks unhappy, what you need to do is match her mood. Sit next to her and say something like, "This party is lousy," then match her facial expression. Now you can commiserate on the lousy dance together and maybe go off and have some fun somewhere else!

Match her choice of the clothing

Match the style and color of the person you wish to attract. She says she is wearing blue? You'll wear blue. She's going cowboy? You wear cowboy. Match the general class of clothing she wears too. I had to bite the bullet and wear the conservative kind of clothing that Jon wore when I was trying to attract him. I disliked "straight" dressing and he liked "yuppie" dressing. But I had to remember my objective; was my goal to attract him or have it my way? Needless to say, it worked and that's why I have been teaching this for nearly ten years.

Matching clothing falls into the category of NLP, or <u>Neuro Linguistic Programming</u> which I discuss in Chapter Eleven. Read that section, then return back here and continue.

If she is a <u>kinesthetic</u>, she's a comfortable dresser and she likes to wear comfortable clothes. So, match her. If you are a visual and dress more neatly than she does, you may intimidate her or turn her off if you are always dressed to kill. Dress down and kick back a little. Try! Loosen up your tie. It's OK to wear a grubby sweatshirt around a kinesthetic. It's OK to have some dirt on your shoes.

If she is a <u>visual</u> and you are a kinesthetic you will need to pay attention to the way you are dressed all the time. Take all your clothes to the dry cleaner. Do NOT press your own shirts; (this is a bad idea no matter what mode your date is in.) Throw out your old clothes or bury them for future dates with kinesthetics. Pay attention to the details. Try to wear the same designer that she does, and dress in the same kind of style. Is she formal? Then you should be formal too. Is she preppy and collegiate? You get the <u>picture</u>. It works like magic or I wouldn't be stressing this. I too had to adapt to being with a visual. As a dyed-in-the-wool kinesthetic it nearly killed me, but it worked, and it will work for you too if you pay attention to this book.

If you are both of the same learning style, it will be no problem. You'll be instantly comfortable around each other and that's why you are trying to match her. You want her to feel comfortable and at ease with you. She doesn't know these techniques, but if you fall in love, you can eventually teach her your modality.

Match her breathing

When you get close to her, you can see the rise and fall of her chest and shoulders. Now match your breathing to her breathing. If you do this during sex, it will be hypnotic and both of you may fall deeply into what people in my business call a trance state. This is a condition where we are more likely to be susceptible to the information that we receive. If she is in this kind of state due to the hypnotic effect of breathing together, she will be more susceptible to remembering your time together as pleasurable. If you are breathing together it certainly will be.

Match her dance style

You can do this when you have just met someone. Is she doing the shag? Then you should try to imitate it. If she's standing still and bouncing, you do the same. Great, she thinks, someone who dances like I dance!

ASSERTIVE MALE BODY LANGUAGE

You read her body language and she reads yours. With the benefit of this book, you will be able to understand what more of her behavior means. However, you also need to look at the way your body signals her and make sure you are sending out assertive, masculine signals. Many of the men I work with have inadvertently developed physical habits that they started doing in response to being shy, feeling uncomfortable, or reacting to verbal or physical abuse in childhood. If you have been criticized, it's natural to want to DUCK to avoid the blow of the words. After years of listening to that kind of abuse, fear can translate into the body posture of hunching. Or, if you felt self-conscious about your height because you shot up quickly, you might have started to hunch to look less conspicuous.

Below, I list some commonly occurring and clearly observable traits which detract a great deal from your appearance.

1. Standing with your shoulders stooped.
2. Standing with your feel turned inwards.
3. Speaking with a slight lisp or in a sped-up, nervous way.
4. Holding your hands in a limp-wristed fashion which can give the appearance of being gay.
5. Speaking too softly (see Chapter Six).
6. Sitting hunched over at a bar or table. Sit tall with your chest back.
7. Habitually turning your head to the side when you talk to a woman and not looking straight at her.

8. Holding your head tilted back when you speak, which gives the impression that you are talking "down your nose" at someone, or that you are stuck up.

9. Sitting with one leg crossed over the other rather than with the right ankle crossed at the left knee. In "sophisticated" circles, or in Britain, knee over knee leg crossing is considered to be fine, but in the United States it also can signal effeminate or gay behavior.

Unfortunately, most people, women as well as men, are not aware of the physical traits that can detract from their appearance and most of our friends are too tactful to give us feedback. A good acting or speech coach can hopefully give you some feedback on any bad habits that you may have. Clinics that specialize in anxiety reduction may be able to give you feedback using videotape analysis. You can also send a video tape to my attention at Island Flower Books and I can give you a personal analysis. See the resource section for more information.

Short of professional advice, the main habits you should learn to cultivate are:

1. Speaking directly and clearly in a normal tone. When in doubt, it is better to be louder than softer.

2. Standing straight with your feet slightly apart; this posture appears strong and assertive. Avoid hunching over, especially if you are tall.

3. Taking up as much space as you can if you are a smaller person. When you are sitting, spread your legs apart, and spread your arms out at your sides or over the back of the couch or adjoining chairs. When you are standing, lean with your arms out on the wall, or the bar, or anything that is available. Try not to stand next to a taller man if you can help it.

4. When you enter a room, stand for a few moments and "survey your territory." This establishes your presence and allows women to get a look at you. Walk slowly and confidently. Let people know that "You're walkin' here!" (Ratso Rizzo in <u>Midnight Cowboy</u>). Exude a confident air. See Chapter Twelve, anxiety reduction techniques to improve your attitude.

The body speaks aloud what we feel inside about ourselves.

Let us hear your body talk.

"She was a lovely girl.
Our courtship was
fast and furious–
I was fast
and she was furious."

—*Max Kauffman*

Pace and 8 Lead

I t's about timing and it's called courtship. Most of the mistakes you may be making with women consist of going too fast or too soon, while a small percentage of you are acting so distant that she can't tell if you care about her or not.

A big misconception about how to go about things is that if it feels good, you should do it. That's kind of like saying, well, I FEEL like a depressed toad, so it's OK to act like one on a date, or, I FEEL like groveling at her feet, so it's a smart thing to do it. A good rule to remember is:

> **Genitals don't think.**

Your genitals merely lead you into a number of wonderful and not so wonderful situations. Perhaps you already know this. If you followed the mood that your "Mr. Happy" was in regularly you'd be in a LOT of trouble. When Mr. Happy sees a great looking woman he wants to run right up to her and INSIST on getting acquainted. Mr. Happy can't think. Your brain can. So, learn to bite the bullet and go at the girl's pace until she's ready for you. Think of it as prolonged foreplay, because that's exactly what it is.

First: Match the pace she takes with you.

Notice what kind of signals she's giving off; read her body language. Is she twisting her fingers into her hair? Is she looking down and up at you? Is she laughing and leaning forward toward you? If she is, there's a good chance that she's attracted to you, so give her a lot of attention at this point. Compliment her; touch her on the arm and hold her hand. Now, watch closely to how she reacts. You never know what she's going to do when you start to touch her. (OK, you never know what she's going to do period, but that's another book.) **Now lead where you want the relationship to go and see if she follows.**

A good way to know if she wants to be affectionate is to try to hold her hand when you are walking somewhere. If she feels uncomfortable, within a minute or at the most two, she will drop your hand. Sometimes she will try to camouflage this by shifting her purse to her other shoulder, or dropping your hand to pick something up. Now she knows that you like her and this puts her in an awkward position if she doesn't yet feel that way about you; so, she tries to be sneaky about how she's feeling. Wait a few minutes, then repeat your attempt. If she drops it again within a fairly short time frame, she's not where you are and you should slow down.

Well, at least now you know how she feels. This is important information and not necessarily a dead end. What you do now is pull back your affection. You pace her. She's not ready? Then you're not ready. Use this concept at all points of the relationship. After she drops your hand you ignore it; a good counter-move is to wander off a little way from her and stop paying attention to her. Appear absorbed in something else. Stop talking with her and focusing on her. Pay attention to yourself for a change. She will notice the shift in your behavior. If she is interested in you, she'll become more talkative and attentive. If not, she'll be relieved.

What you are doing here is matching her interest level in the romantic relationship. What most men do when the woman isn't interested is to speed up their attentions. They try even harder. This is not sexy behavior—it's dweeby behavior.

PACE: Match her interest level in the relationship.

LEAD: Push the envelope a little. Ask for more. She's not ready? Back off and start over with pacing

Another example? You've had a first date. You call her up and ask her out again for Saturday. She waffles. You counter with a second, less important night, she waffles again. STOP NOW. Don't ask her out for coffee if she is "busy" both nights. Third times the charm is OK before you get a date, and are trying the "ask three times" maneuver, but not after she's actually gone out with you once. If she really wants to see you after you suggest two possible date times, she will suggest an alternate day and her tone will be apologetic. If she doesn't counter, tell her you'll catch her later when her schedule isn't so—BUSY, implying indirectly through your amused tone that you know she's trying to get out of it.

Don't appear fazed. Hold your chin up! A champion doesn't sweat in front of a lady until he's in bed with her. . . .DON'T ask her why she doesn't have time or what else she is doing with some other guy. It will only make you look weak. Instead, disappear for a week or so. Don't call her. This is the time for you to call all the other women that you are interested in. You say you don't have any other women you're interested in? Well, get some quick, or you'll feel strung out every time a girl doesn't want to be with you. You'll start to feel like a loser and possibly desperate.

<u>Keep three eggs in your hat, if one breaks you'll have two more.</u> Simply replace the egg that got away with another

one as soon as possible. This concept has worked for every one of my male clients and it worked for me. Because if you only have one egg that you're interested in, you'll stand over it and shout:

HATCH! HATCH! I LOVE YOU LITTLE EGG!
COME TO PAPA!

And that little egg sits there thinking, "I'm not comin' out if my life depends on it."

She feels you BREATHING down her neck, feels you wanting, wanting, WANTING her and she feels suffocated.

Get back, Jack! Think back on good old Betty who chased you around, baked you cookies, called you, wrote you notes, even showed up at your work weeping. Very appealing— Not. Isn't it the pits that we are attracted to people who act like we don't exist? So, you need to let her know that you're not going to just hang around and take seconds. You have a life! (Go get one now.)

Some Direct Examples of Pacing:

- You've been dating once a week for three weeks? Now you move the frequency up to twice a week. Call her once in between times, but don't become a doormat and certainly don't call her every day!

- You're dating three times a week? She's really yours now. But should you be seeing each other every day? No. Should you let some days pass when you don't call her or see her? Definitely yes. (See the section on "Intermittent Reinforcement" in Chapter Eleven.)

  You want to spend Christmas with her and she hasn't brought it up or hinted around? Make plans to do something else. If she really, really, wants to be with you, you can cancel them, right? Because it is possible that she was waiting for <u>you</u> to ask.

Close to the time when you absolutely need to decide, if she hasn't given you some hints, you say something like, "What are you planning to do for the holidays?" If she says, "Well, uh, I don't know, what're <u>you</u> going to do," this means that she wants to be with you and wants you to suggest something. If she says that she plans to fly to Detroit to see her parents or she has tickets to Greece, you're out of luck. You say, "Too bad, I was hoping we'd have some time together." She might make an alternate suggestion at that point. If she doesn't, now is the time to look elsewhere.

- She pulls away when you are close to making love? That's when you hold back. Stop trying to take her clothes off or touch her body. It won't work until she's ready, (see Chapter Ten.)

Examples of Bad Pacing

- At the end of a date, you tell her you had a great time and really want to see her again, how about tomorrow night? Too soon.

- You send her a dozen roses after your second date. Too fast, unless you've had sex with her. (**And then, you absolutely must send them.**)

- On the first date, you tell her about the great trips you're going to take her on. You talk to her as if you are already crazy about her. This implies a lack of discrimination on your part. HOLD BACK until at least a month has passed.

- You make love with her. Then you disappear and don't call. **This is grounds for murder.** Don't do this unless your goal is to dump her.

- She tells you how she feels about you, but you remain quiet about how you feel. Initially this may work to intrigue her, and it's a good idea if you have been used to overdoing it, but you must find something positive and truthful to respond with and match her willingness to be open to keep her feeling good.

- You are in the initial stages of courtship and it's beginning to heat up. She sends you cards and notes and you don't give her anything. Ouch!

ABOUT RISK

Someone has to take that final plunge sooner or later. Luckily for you, most women who are genuinely interested in a guy will start showing significant OBVIOUS signs that they are interested. For those of you who need a clue:

Ten signs that show she really likes you.

1. She phones you when you don't phone her.
2. She asks you where you've been if you don't call according to your regular pattern.
3. She cooks for you.
4. She calls you honey and other pet names.
5. She likes to kiss you and give you physical attention.
6. She gets upset if you forget special occasions.
7. She melts like butter when you send her flowers.
8. She asks you to go out; she buys the tickets.
9. She get angry and frustrated, has fits or cries.
10. She is exceedingly happy at the little things you do for her.

Decide whether she is interested in you based on these ten signs. Are you throwing away time that could be better spent on a woman who would appreciate you? After working with thousands of men and women I can give you a general time frame. If you have been dating her off and on for a good two months and she's not willing to spend more time with you, hasn't been significantly affectionate, or doesn't show any of the above signs, she probably isn't really interested in you.

If she's dating someone else that she likes better, or "you just aren't her type," cut your losses and move on.

I know that some of you are CONVINCED that this woman is worth the pain and heartache, that <u>you</u> are the one who will wear her down. Here are some thoughts on what you are doing:

- Sacrificing your own self-esteem in an attempt to gain love repeats the messages you learned in childhood such as:

  "If I just try hard enough to please them, Mom and Dad will love me."

  "Love is hard and difficult."

  "I have to work to get love."

- You are giving to her what you want her to give to you.

- You don't feel worthy of a woman who can really love you, so you unconsciously choose a woman whose treatment of you matches this unworthiness.

Push the envelope

There is a <u>small</u>, remote possibility that she does want you. She might just be playing a fierce game of hard to get, or else you aren't very good at seeing the signs. Or, sometimes you will both be trying to hold out to avoid rejection. It's time to get direct.

- Wait no more than two months, in case you are going faster than you think you are.

- Then be direct with her. Tell her you want to spend more time with her; come right out and ask her for that big event. Ask her how she feels about the relationship, where does she see it going?

- If she waffles and is non-committal after this frank talk, again, pay attention to what she is <u>doing</u>. Is she letting you touch her? If so, assume that she is still interested. Most women don't make love right away, so don't use that as a signpost.

If you can't see the signs, and she isn't touching you, but is continuing to go out with you, she either:

1. Doesn't want the relationship, but likes the money you spend on her.

2. Is very ambivalent about commitment. Don't expect this resistant behavior to change anytime soon.

3. Has been burned and is holding back on purpose. If you choose her, you are choosing this kind of psychological defense. Don't expect this to change without counseling.

What can happen if you don't let her know you like her.

Frankly, my dear, she will leave you if she's smart. If you hold back from showing your feelings because you are afraid of being hurt, because you aren't quite getting what you want, you had better deal with this habit and quick. You are playing come and get me and you may lose her. Maybe you got hurt in the past and you don't want to get hurt again. Life has no guarantees. Someone usually gets hurt. But no risk, no reward, remember? I suggest you see a counselor if this tendency has sabotaged your other relationships; you could die a lonely camper.

<u>Did you know that single men are much more likely to die of heart failure than married men, or men who live with a partner?</u>

It's time to take a risk. If you watch for the signs that she really likes you and they are there, you have a good chance of getting a commitment from her. If you really want her, tell her how you feel...

For those of you out there who are hedging your bets, fearing rejection, I leave you with this quote:

" Life is either a daring adventure or nothing" —Hellen Keller

---

"Clothes gave us individuality, distinctions; clothes have made men of us."

—*Thomas Carlyle*

Your Clothes, Face and Body: How Women View You

9

n article in the *Seattle Times* commented about something I discuss in the men's classes I teach, specifically, the female habit of judging a man by the quality of his shoes. Eighty percent of all the women agreed with all of the things I said including this particular point. How did I discover this underground secret? Well, I had a close girlfriend who once told me that if a guy's shoes didn't look good to her she wouldn't go out with him. At the time, I thought this was pretty extreme. As there is no research available regarding shoe preference in dating, I have been taking informal polls in my classes and seminars about several personal appearance items and classy men's shoes are high on the list.

Speaking of class, the type of clothing you wear reveals you to be of a certain socio-economic level. If you dress blue collar, you will attract women from the blue collar class. Of course, this can work the opposite way too. If you are a blue collar type of guy, you may be unimpressed by white collar dressing. But men are usually attracted to pretty women everywhere no matter what they have on. If she's not attracted to you, consider how you are dressed. Dress a class up and you will attract wealthier, prettier women. If you get caught at the filling station looking grubby, and bump into Miss Right, it's important to imply as soon as possible that you have a good job. Try to joke about your grubby appearance, and use your charisma to overcome your clothes. "You've caught me slumming —at least now you know I can change a tire." Or offer to take her to dinner at an nice restaurant to counterbalance your appearance. Despite all our good intentions, people judge us by our outward appearance.

Women agree that they do look at and judge men by their shoes. While shoes are not deal breakers for all women, they are status *cues* to a lot of us. Some shoes look nerdy, while other shoes spell *class*. Other accessories like belts and ties should be of the highest quality leather and silk that you can afford. Socks should be thin for business, and in a tone to match your suit, shoes or tie. If you don't know how to do this, check out *Esquire*, or other men's magazines, like *Details*, *GQ*, *Men's Health* and *Playboy* and ask a men's store clerk to help you duplicate the look. If you have the money, hire a wardrobe consultant.

The other day, one of my clients bought some expensive dress loafers. He usually wears practical, budget-conscious shoes. At my men's group, where we discuss and practice these things, he told us that several women at work had noticed and highly approved of his new shoes. Are his shoes going to make a difference in getting girls to go out with him? Maybe not, but they gave him one more bargaining tool, a second look, which he used to influence the women of his choice.

Robert Cialdini's excellent book *Influence: The Psychology of Persuasion* discusses the effect of a uniform or a doctor's diploma on the wall. A friend tells me that in Los Angeles, men ostentatiously display their Ferrari keys in front of the women they want to impress. Another friend told me a story about receiving the royal treatment in an English pub because he happened to be driving an infamous Bentley which actually belonged to his uncle, a famous jockey. The pub owner was angry to discover that he offered free drinks to the wrong person. Like the uniform, diploma or Bentley, the way you dress influences women. So, do *you* want to attract low-budget, cheap women? If you aren't dressed well, you will be dismissed by higher class women who, more often than not, are thinner and take better care of themselves than women in the lower classes.

Women generally like well-dressed men. The "exceptional few" aren't so quick to judge. I love looking at casually dressed men and I don't discount them. I do, however, look for *other* signs of status if a man is dressed casually, like nice tennis shoes. I hope you don't discount women for the way they are dressed either. In most parts of the United States, women feel uncomfortable wearing miniskirts and figure-revealing clothes; men sometimes think the wearer is "loose." Try not to stereotype people, but be aware of the effect these gatekeepers have on all of us.

The way you dress effects how masculine the woman finds you to be. And if there's one trigger women are attracted to it's masculine dressing. I have developed a method to help men dress in a way that makes them look bigger, taller, and more broad-shouldered, the masculine signals. Here are the basics:

IF YOU ARE SHORT OR HAVE A SLIGHT BUILD

Wear white or light colors: white, beige, camels, light blues and greens all the time. Your pants and shirts should be in the same tone, which makes you look taller. Wear the lightest color, like a white shirt, on the top. White always makes your chest look bigger. <u>Do not wear dark colors at all.</u>

About patterns

Horizontal stripes will make you look broader and bigger. If worn across the chest or shoulders in a bright color, you'll look larger. If worn across the chest in a dark color, you will look smaller. Don't wear horizontal stripes anywhere near any area like your stomach that is paunchy. If the stripe on the shirt is above the chest, and everything below it is a dark color, this camouflages pretty well.

Vertical stripes will make you look taller and slender. If you are short, wear vertical stripes that are broader.

Consider the following picture:

Which set of lines appears narrower?
Which appears wider?

Each set of lines is the same dimension, yet they appear not to be because of the direction of the lines. Take a look at these pictures:

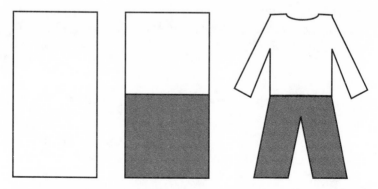

Which box appears to be larger?

If you wear a dark pair of pants on the bottom, and a light shirt on the top, you will look shorter.

Other Tips for Shorter Guys

Don't wear horizontal lines of any kind if you are short. Don't wear a black belt, as it can help cut your height in half. Even buckles across your shoes can make your feet look small. Wear loafers or shoes with clean lines, no cuffs on your pants, and avoid long jackets

TIPS FOR THE OVERWEIGHT

Wear black, navy blue, dark green, olive. The darker the color the better. You will look smaller. No horizontal stripes, no white at all, no bright colors or loud patterns. Do not cinch your belt under your stomach so that your stomach protrudes over the belt. Women don't like it. And if you wear a large belt buckle, you'll draw everyone's attention there. Don't wear tight pants which can give you a "wedgie." Don't wear jackets that give you bulk, like ski jackets with puffy sleeves. Try the over-hanging shirt look and don't tuck it in at all. Wear thin ties that are dark, and loosen your tie up. Severely overweight people look better without a tie. And double-breasted suits don't look good on you, only single-breasted in a dark color and be sure to button your jacket, don't wear it open.

TIPS FOR THE TALL AND SLENDER

First of all, stand up straight! Yes, your mama knew best. You look terrible all slumped over! You need to try to put some weight on your chest and bulk up by weight lifting. Wear lighter colors on the top and try to get shirts with horizontal stripes across the chest and shoulders. Shirts with fullness in the sleeves will make you look broader. No turtle necks, tight shirts or "v" necks. This will accentuate your thinness. You can get away with about any color pants, but lighter is best. A vest will make you look even thinner. You can also wear wider ties, and you can get away with checks or loud patterns. Unbutton your jacket to add width. Overly large "pirate shirts" in white with a lot of fabric in the chest and sleeves create heft. Try these.

ABOUT HAIR AND SHAPE
AND DIMENSION OF YOUR FACE

If you have a small face, you should shave off your beard and mustache. What? You like them? Well, <u>did you know that most women prefer smooth-shaven men</u>? This is because romantic love is linked to the mothering instinct (remember when you call her <u>baby</u>? It's the same idea.) So, the baby-faced man usually gets more women. Think Paul McCartney. And if you have a small face and are wearing a mustache, the horizontal mustache line cuts your face in half and makes you look smaller. If you have a long narrow face, a horizontal mustache will probably work. If you have a large, broad face, you can get away with a mustache and a beard. If you are wearing glasses, AND a mustache, AND a beard, you are completely covering up your features. Come out to play!

May I remind you guys that most of you prefer long hair on women and when they cut it they don't look as feminine? Of course, you have to say that you like it when they ask, but does that mean you really do? No. Well, women feel the same way about your facial hair and your glasses; they just don't tell you. Of course, now you'll go out and ask all the women you know, and they'll say they LOVE your mustache. Well, ask them if you should shave it. If they immediately say NO they love it . . . maybe they are part of the "exceptional few." But, if they waffle, they want to see you without it. Of all the men who have shaved their mustaches after taking my class, (perhaps sixty) only <u>one</u> looked better with it.

Making yourself look attractive to women means developing a certain style to your clothing that looks as masculine as possible. To achieve this, I dress men in the style that can send the most masculine image, which is often **the opposite of how they are currently dressing**. People usually dress according to their personalities. A guy who is a loud mouth often wears bright colors, a blue collar guy will wear casual sweatshirts and ratty tennis shoes and most engineers wears drab looking clothes that have no sex appeal whatsoever—and, in general the most awful looking shoes! Do you engineers out there want to be functional to the point of never getting a date?

IF YOU ARE MILD-MANNERED INTELLECTUAL TYPE,

have a slight build or a shy attitude, I would put you in <u>athletic looking clothes</u>: preppy clothes, outdoorsy or rugged-looking clothes, layered looks like two or three shirts worn on top of each other, varsity jackets, black motorcycle jackets, jean jackets, plaid wool jackets with bulk, bright, primary colors like blues, reds, greens (depending on your coloring of course), high-end tennis shoes and hiking boots and <u>nothing that is drab or subdued</u> (the opposite of introverted.) <u>Nautica</u> is a good line for you to consider. Take off your black calculator watch! Get a gold one or one with a leather band. If you are still wearing "engineer" glasses that have a straight bar over the brim of your nose, upgrade to the latest style. Try tortoise shell frames. If you have a small face, get contacts, and shave your beard and mustache. <u>In short, you need to look like you are an athletic jock</u>. Do not worry that you "aren't being yourself." <u>Is yourself attracting women</u>? Your superior brain will help balance out any obnoxious masculine signals which will be sent by this sexy dressing. . .

OTHER MASCULINE CLOTHING CUES

- Western clothes.
- Cowboy boots.
- Leather sleeveless vests.
- Denim jackets.
- White shirts and ties.
- Soft flannel shirts.
- The *Eddie Bauer* look (outdoor men's clothing store).
- Shirts with emblems.

- Suspenders, on a nicely built man (make sure they connect to the pants with buttons, not clasps, and if you're thin don't wear them).
- Loosening up your tie a <u>little</u> bit.

IF YOU ARE A BLUE COLLAR WORKING GUY

You need to dress <u>up</u> a class. Your shoes should cost over a hundred easily. Your shirts should be dry cleaned with a little starch. Always wear a tie. In general, spend money on your clothes. Get the men's magazines and look at what they are wearing. Duplicate the look. You are competing, unfortunately, with the white collar crowd for the same pretty women. This is because women usually prefer men with money. Yes, I <u>know</u> many of you do better than business types—but the <u>majority</u> of you usually don't. Use your body to your advantage. Shirts that are a <u>little</u> tight in the chest are fine if you've got that kind of build. And if you can still wear snug fitting jeans, (meaning you don't have a "pot,") we LIKE that. Make sure your fingernails are clean and your socks are thin. You can wear your cowboy boots as long as they are made from real leather.

IF YOU WANT TO LOOK OLDER

No T-shirts, no penny loafers, no varsity jackets or sweatshirts with clever sayings. Wear polo shirts, a nice look is layered in different colors. Polos also look good under a jacket. No buckles on your shoes and avoid tennis shoes. Think lean and mean. Black, dangerous dressing is best—stay away from baby blues and soft colors. And comb your hair straight off your forehead instead of wearing it down on your forehead. Ghoatees can make you look more sophisticated.

SOME GENERAL GUIDELINE ABOUT DRESS ITEMS:

1. Don't wear business shoes with jeans.
2. A sign of a quality shoe is that the heels are made from layered leather and the stitching is smooth, the lining is soft, no glue is showing, they bend easily, then go back into shape.

3. Let your good shoes breathe a day between wearing them; use wooden shoe trees.

4. When wearing a business suit, the shoes should be no lighter in color than the suit.

5. Socks should be high enough not to show your skin. Never wear dress socks that bag.

6. Wear thick socks with casual clothes, thin socks for business. Never wear bulky socks with dress clothes.

7. Wearing no socks is sexy with loafers, moccasins or Sperry Topsiders.

8. Avoid jaunty English caps with bills. This isn't England.

9. Long overcoats and cashmere scarves are a class act.

10. Women still think that small bags shouldn't be carried by a man. In fact, they used to be called "fag bags!"

11. When matching ties, the tie should follow the shirt color, then match the rest of the accessories.

12. The collar frames the face. A narrow face looks good in a high one, but avoid long collars and thin ties. A broad face looks better in a low collar that just covers the breast bone. To get your collar size, measure your neck below the Adam's apple, and put one finger inside the tape. It should fit snugly.

13. Never be without the best white shirt you can buy. They are usually made from super fine cotton. Less formal shirts have a rougher weave. Most women are crazy for men in white shirts that are starched.

14. Pant length should be just above the shoe, slightly exposing the sock, but it is considered higher class when the pants rest on the shoes, cuffs or no cuffs.

15. Watch for frayed cuffs and collars. When you go to pick out a tie, check out the one they have on the dummy, they usually use the best one there, and they will sell it to you.

16. Never buy a tie from a man who is considerably older than you are, unless you're under twenty-five. He'll pick out one that looks dated that HE likes.

17. Pick the sharpest dressed guy that is closest to your age to wait on you. He'll dress you better.

18. Remember that dressing for women is different than dressing for fashion.

BASIC RULES TO FOLLOW

- Accentuate your chest. Try to get it to look like a "V" shape.

- Use optical illusion to make yourself look the best you can.

- Buy the best shoes and ties you can afford.

- Buy less but buy a higher quality, it will last longer and look better.

- Keep your jewelry understated. Heavy gold chains are not considered sexy these days—only in some places, notably in the southern half of the U.S. Heavy gold chains around the neck (especially with a medallion attached to it) went out in the seventies. You can usually get away with a thin turquoise bracelet. Remember the more artistic you look, the more women you will rule out; you want to appeal to the MOST amount of women. If you're under thirty, leather around the wrist and neck is fine, but not in conservative business environments. And nose rings, well...

HYGIENE

If no one has told you that you have bad breath or body odor, that doesn't mean that you don't have it! Ask one of your close friends who has been around you. If you feel comfortable, ask a co-worker, especially the guy who works right next to you. Start out by saying something like, "You know that guy Fred in accounting? Well, boy he stinks. I hope, if I have bad breath that someone tells me. What do you think,—do I have bad breath?" Maybe he will let you know then and there but probably not. It is not socially acceptable to tell anyone that they have bad breath or body odor. And so, what happens? This poor guy walks around all the time not knowing. One dead giveaway is that people literally *back away* from you when you get close. Another way to take care of body odor is the obvious—shower daily, and wear deodorant. But bad breath often occurs with a nervous stomach, so carry a breath spray if you are out trying to meet women for the first time.

Also, invest in a good smelling cologne. Women love it. If you wear the same brand all the time, when she smells it, she'll think of you. The sense of smell is the oldest sense, and some say the most powerful.

GROOMING

Haines Ely, M.D., Professor of Dermatology at U.C. Davis, California gives us the following perspective:

I'm a bald guy so I'm going to get right to the point and talk about hair loss. Believe it or not, the guys who worry about hair the most are those who have plenty of it. Many men identify who they are with their hair. At the first sign of thinning at the temples or hair on the shower floor they begin to suffer self- image problems.

I used to say "I am not my hair" and yet I behaved as if I were. This is an act. We're all on the planet acting out roles - hair is part of the costume. It is part of our presentation of who we are. We all "act." Kindness is an act. Intelligence is an act. Power, charisma, confidence, laziness, or any other trait we present to the world are all acts. We are capable of a full range of being yet we categorize and label ourselves into a narrow pattern of action.

As a man loses his hair he compares what he knows about baldness to his standard act, then modifies his behavior to fit the pattern he associates with baldness. He sees the likes of Goldfinger, Churchill, Patrick Stewart, or Sean Connery and they stand out as rich, powerful, charismatic. In regard to hair our act becomes very dramatic. Drama calls attention to ourselves. We want to make a difference. We want to know we are loved and lovable. The balding man thinks others are looking at him and judging him because of his hair loss and that the judgment will be less harsh if he has hair. In reality nobody cares!

The acts, drama, and judgments of balding men cannot be eliminated but they can be transcended. Dr. Clark has pointed out that women are attracted to financially secure and powerful men. Baldness is often associated with these qualities (as we compensate for lowered self-esteem by over-achieving). I remember a letter to Ann Landers from a bus driver who said in all his years driving in the Bowery he never saw a bald bum. This says something about how baldness alters human behavior. When we can love and accept ourselves exactly as we are (and are not) there is no need to act. I can be myself with nothing added. I can tell the truth about my behavior.

How has hair affected your presentation to the world? What has it done to the way you think about yourself? Tell the truth. When you begin to examine who you really are it may be scary. Few people have the courage to see if their life matters. If your love life is somehow connected to your hair, or lack of it, you are unable to see your act clearly. Are you trying by some tricky hair style to hide behind your costume? No one is fooled by the "comb one hair all over the top of the head" hairstyle. Drop it.

My best advice from personal experience: Give up your bald act now. It is not you. It never was you. Don't cheat yourself out of knowing who you really are. Be vulnerable. Be available for the people around you. Let them know who you really are. If you're balding, flaunt it. Cut the hair short.

About hair transplants. Good hair transplants are expensive (figure ten grand as a low price), but most men aren't candidates for quality results. It takes dense hair with a slight curl to it for the best outcome. Most bald guys don't have this type of hair in the donor sites. A hair transplant is done with a round knife, just like a cookie cutter. One cuts a round plug bearing hairs from the side of the head and inserts it into a hole created where one wants the hair to grow. Just like cookies on a baking sheet, there are spaces between the circles. These are quite obvious. The frontal hairline looks awful unless one inserts tinier and tinier plugs into the spaces between the larger plugs. This area gets the most attention. With aging continued hair loss causes the plugs behind the frontal hairline to be more and more obvious. Eventually the transplant looks like a Taiwanese kewpie doll and everyone notices it. Same goes for toupees. Women hate them. They don't fool anyone.

Be yourself with nothing added. No armor. No protection. Make your life matter. Confront your own negative thoughts and see what's underneath the act. Your true self is under all this stuff. Aliveness and full expression are under the fears. Joy and energy are there too. Aliveness and emotional expression attract women more than all the hair on a Yeti. Behave as if baldness were a magnet for women. It is. Women often say among themselves that bald men make the best lovers. They do. As Eddy "Clean Head" Vincent once said: "All the pretty girls running their fingers through it wore my hair off." Love yourself and accept yourself exactly as you are.

For those of you who have too much hair: keep it well groomed and clean. Shampoo every day. Hair and nails are both dead tissue. There is nothing which can "revitalize" hair or add protein or anything else to it. Simple soaps or shampoos are adequate. Dandruff shampoos are rarely necessary if one shampoos daily. Sebum (skin oil) on the scalp becomes rancid and releases fatty acids which cause itching and flaking. Frequently washing away the scalp oil will not promote hair loss or any other problem. Conditioners are simply glues which hold the frayed ends of the hair together. Men rarely if ever need a conditioner unless they have very long hair. Don't spend money on fancy shampoos or conditioners. Don't ever use hairspray unless you wear a diamond stick pin and a Rolex watch on your TV outreach ministry.

Nails

Women look at men's hands and shoes. Odd eh? Dirty fingernails or dirt imbedded in every crack of the skin appeal only to the women who love manual laborers. You may be the best diesel mechanic in the world but you only have one chance to make a first impression. If one has to work in grease or heavy dirt either wear gloves or use a silicone barrier hand cream such as Kerodex or Wonder Gloves to keep dirt from sticking. Cut the nails short, keep them clean. Whitening or thickening of the nails is often a fungus infection. Your M.D. can cure this easily with an oral antifungal medication.

COSMETIC SURGERY FOR MEN

This information is provided by Susan L. Clark, Image Consultant. She has appeared on national media regarding cosmetic surgery and its positive outcomes and her computer imaging photos have been published nationally. She works closely with Dr. Jim Billie of *The Cosmetic Surgery Center* in Little Rock, Arkansas. See the *Resource Section* for more details.

Dr. Billie is a Harvard graduate with both a dental and medical degree. He currently serves as one of the Oral Board Examiners for the *American Board of Cosmetic Surgery.* He is on the editorial staff of the *American Journal of Cosmetic Surgery,* and is Board Certified by the *American Board of Cosmetic Surgery* and *The American Board of Otolaryngology.* Dr. Billie is known the world over for his work on beauty pageant contestants and celebrities.

As an image consultant for the past ten years with Dr. Jim Billie, my experiences have been more than interesting, and yes, men have made up a part of that experience. Although the percentage of female patients is higher, the number of male patients increases every year, Why? The reasons are simple: more affordable, more available, and the results are more predictable and, in general, more acceptable than ever before. It is obvious to state that as more women become "enhanced" with cosmetic surgery procedures, their significant others: husbands, sons, brothers, fathers, and even grandfathers fall into line! Men want to look better too, and as the "clock is being turned back" on their wives and/or girlfriends, these men certainly don't want to be left behind looking like "last year's model"!

What cosmetic surgery procedures are these men opting for in order to get in step with what the world needs now? Well, that depends on their age. Men in their twenties generally opt for the nose job (usually a sports related injury), chin liposuction, and chin implant. These can all be done in one surgical setting or separately depending on the need. And let's not forget the ears. If they stick out, we can flatten them back! The big nose and the "fly away" ears are usually corrected because of childhood teasing, a powerful wound to the psyche.

With hair loss, the "cure" by hair transplant has come a long way. With the right surgeon, miracles can happen. But, with the wrong surgeon, it can be disastrous! There is nothing, and I do mean nothing, uglier than a bad hair transplant! And they are very difficult to correct, if not impossible. Once those clumps are planted, it's nearly impossible to make the hair look natural. I've seen many young men with long, sad faces and "baby doll" roots on their heads hoping that Dr. Billie could undo the damage of another surgeon's hands. Part of the trauma here is the female turn-off factor. There is no bigger turn-off to a woman than a bad hair transplant. I knew a girl who went on a boating date, and when the boat started speeding down the lake, she looked over at her date only to see the wind blowing his hair back and exposing the most bodacious hair plugs she had ever seen! She was so repulsed that he had to take her home. Fortunately, we have come "a long way baby" from that procedure.

Along with hair loss, men in their thirties and forties seem to focus on aging, baggy eyelids and the dreaded "love-handles". The upper and lower eyelid surgery does take away that tired appearance and some men have opted for laser skin resurfacing around the lower eyelid and crow's feet area. It is an amazing outcome when all three procedures are done together, for years are erased from the face. Sometimes even vision is improved if the upper eyelids are impinging on their vision—and with Dr. Billy's techniques, the eyelids don't look fake, as if they did not even match the rest of the face. You have to remember, there is a delicate balance between looking "refreshed" versus "overdone".

And what about those guys who work out several days a week but just can't shake that spare tire? Liposuction is the answer. And believe it or not, our men are the best patients in recovery; they seem to snap back quicker than the women. We're not sure why, because, as we all know, men are usually not the best patients. If that fat is still hanging around after diligent work-outs and proper dieting, it's not going away without liposuction. These men care enough about their appearance to get to the gym and have no compunction about having a few fat cells sucked out. It works! They love it!

One year we had several servicemen come in for liposuction of the waist area. They were up for their yearly measurements to maintain military status and were concerned that they might not make the cut. Dr. Billie reduced all of their waists by several inches and they all passed with flying colors—a happy group!

I remember one gentleman that wasn't so happy. He was a nationally known CEO with a portly mid-section. Being a multi-millionaire, money was certainly no object to stand in the way of the svelte physique he imagined he could have. He was a big and powerful man, warm and kind with a childlike excitement. We talked about every detail of the surgery and he waited anxiously for Dr. Billie to come in for the final approval. The doctor examined his abdomen, only to declare that his fat was omental. That is, on the inside of the abdominal wall and therefore, liposuction would not work for him. I couldn't help but feel sad as he left.

But then there was our Mr. Jones, whose dream became a reality. He was in his early sixties and a grandfather to a seven year-old girl. One day they were talking and she told him he looked like an iguana. He asked her why and she said because the skin on his neck was so saggy. Well, that was all it took to get him to see Dr. Billie. Grandma came too and was totally supportive. I put him on the computer imager and drew the image he would become with Dr. Billie's magic hands. They were both elated. Even his wife, who had never had cosmetic surgery was excited. As I erased the "iguana" neckline, Mr. Jones' eyes began to light up and it was clear there was no turning back. That precious grand-daughter was his impetus for change, and change he did. He emerged a different man. After face lift, upper and lower eyelid surgery and laser around his eyes, "grandpa" was looking more like "Dad". Fifteen years had been swept from his face and his spirits were uplifted. Later, I asked him if his granddaughter had noticed the change, and he said she hadn't mentioned it, but that was OK. After all, the only iguana she'll be seeing now will probably be a Beanie Baby.

So what do men really want when it come to cosmetic surgery? First of all, they will usually say they are doing it for someone else. And that's OK, because a part of their motivation might be that, but the other part is nurturing the insecurity that is ever present in those small hidden corners of their hearts. Younger men just want to look better and older men want to look as good as they feel. And we all want to be loved and accepted regardless of what imperfections prevail.

Susan Clark, with Dr. Jim Billie
Little Rock Cosmetic Surgery Center
"Helping You Look Better is What We Do Best"

Diane Keaton:

"Sex without love is meaningless."

Woody Allen:

"Yes, but as meaningless experiences go, it's one of the best."

Sexual 10 Dominance

After putting to good use all the other behaviors I've been suggesting, maybe you're finally getting regular dates and some affection. But, like most guys, you've just been *reading* this book off and on and probably haven't been *doing* anything. This chapter is about how to enjoy sexual pleasure after you have managed to get women close to you by (let me repeat) *doing the things* I suggest. You may be relieved to know that once a woman actually decides to make love with you, she will want you again *if you can maintain an emotional connection with her.* If you act like a jerk and don't call her the next day, you are in for trouble.

My friend Emmy had a serious romance with a man who could not sustain his erections—ever. Despite this, she said she enjoyed the lovemaking because he was very cuddly and knew how to please her in other ways. After about eight months she grew tired of the relationship, but it was <u>not</u> because of his inability to sustain erections; it was because of his inability to commit. This is a no-brainer to a woman; we are far more interested in being held, kissed and loved up than in how long you can keep it up.

HOW TO GET WHAT YOU REALLY WANT

Wait until she has given you obvious signs that she wants you to get physical. Here are the signs:

- She might pull on your jacket, lean against you, or grab your hand. You see her playing with her hair, bouncing her leg, looking down, then up at you in a coy, girlish fashion. She will escalate this type of behavior until you give her some physical affection. Women who want to be touched always give these physical signals! She'll nudge you, poke you, brush up against you, touch your arm or hand or even sit in your lap without an invitation. She'll practically throw themselves at you if they become frustrated enough. **This is what you want her to do. You do not want her to pull away because you come on too fast.**

You want her to want it

Don't try to go for the gold right away or you will alienate her. And no, she won't leave you if you wait before making your move. As long as you don't wait too long. I know, HOW LONG IS TOO LONG? A safe bet is that if you haven't tried to kiss her in three dates, she'll wonder what's up. But she won't think you're gay, that's a locker-room myth. She will think *more* highly of you if you wait. Remember, she is testing you not only for your assertive personality, but for your ability to be emotionally nurturing. If you rush things, or constantly push for sex, she will categorize you as a jerk, or at the least insensitive. The problem with going too fast is that it will take you even longer to warm her up the second time, and who wants to waste time?

- If you try to kiss her and she freezes up, it's a sign that she isn't ready. It does not mean she won't *ever* be ready! Calm down. Watch for a few dates and read her body language. If she gives you non-verbal signals by touching you more and more, it's OK to kiss her. *Before you get to this point, confine your physical advances to holding hands or gently putting your hand on her back now and then.*

■ Sometimes, a woman will spontaneously hug you at the end of the date. This could be a "let's just be friends" hug, or a sign that she wants more. Test this out. After you hug her, if she doesn't pull away, then kiss her once very gently. If she backs away quickly, or gives you the cheek, this is not a good sign. But, if she smiles, leans against you, or lingers, she probably wants more. Go ahead and give her a deeper, longer kiss.

■ Eye contact during this period is crucial—it establishes an emotional connection. It assures your friend that you see her, not just her body. (Oh, come on, you have too noticed <u>something</u> else!)

■ After you have dated her two or three times, if she doesn't show signs of touching you more, try to kiss her and see how she reacts. If she gives you the cold fish and pulls away, or she is not showing any of the non-verbal behaviors I list in Chapter Seven like leaning against you—sorry, but nine times out of ten, it's because ***SHE IS NOT INTERESTED IN YOU.*** She may continue to go out with you because:

1. She is lonely
2. You are a convenient meal ticket
3. You are good at rescuing her
4. She's afraid she'll hurt you when she dumps you

You say that you think she will come around in time and leave her boyfriend? You *believe* that when she gets through her "busy work schedule" or comes back from France that she'll see you and it's been six months? Well, if she isn't kissing you, holding your hand and letting you put your arm around her by three or four dates, you have very little possibility that it will ever happen. GET A CLUE, as the jerk likes to say. A doormat loves to hang around, buy the girl dinner, let her break dates and hope, hope, hope that she will appreciate him. You have other "friends" don't you? Friends you don't want to sleep with? Stop torturing yourself! The more you let her treat you like a *friend*, the less likely she will ever see you as a *lover*. Remember:

FRIEND IS ANOTHER WORD FOR NO SEX

Moving right along . . . .

So things are warming up?

So you think you've got a chance?

Not unless you consider the following. . . .

Have You Directly Discussed AIDS, Herpes, and Condoms Beforehand?

Many women will not make love with you unless those issues have been discussed *in advance*, and some women will view you negatively if <u>you</u> don't bring them up. It's common now for people to openly discuss their sexual histories before deciding to proceed. Do NOT suddenly decide to have this discussion when you are rolling around on the floor!. . . A turn-off to say the least! If you don't want this yucky discussion to interfere, have it at a neutral location far in advance. **And don't always believe <u>her</u> innocent sexual history just because she <u>says</u> so** as she bats her baby blues. Do *you* plan on telling *her* about that lurid affair you had last month? Carry condoms. Don't act stupid and die. <u>It is not only her responsibility to deal with it, it's yours</u>. See the end of this chapter on condoms, HIV and disease.

You need to spend several dates making out in various and nefarious kinds of places.

<u>Try to avoid having your kissing sessions at her house or your house</u>. While *you* are thinking, "Boy, I'd like to do the deed with her," *she* is thinking, "How am I going to get out it?" or, "I'd really *like* to have sex with him, but I'm not going to let him do it any time soon." How can anyone enjoy getting sexy when they are planning political strategy? So, until she gives you the definite go-ahead, do your necking and foreplay somewhere else!

Do it in the car. If your girl is over thirty, chances are good that the car is one good place she fooled around when she was younger. Rev up those memories by going parking in some secluded spot. Play the music she enjoyed when she was younger. It works like magic. Do the math—what was popular when she was seventeen? ("Twentieth Century Fox" by The Doors worked real well with your author.) All of us have powerful memories of our first sexual experiences, and the music we listened to during those early cavortings. And don't forget to take her to the places that fit with her "primary mode," whether visual, auditory, or kinesthetic, (see Chapter Eleven.)

For those of you who need any reminders, here's the short form of what MOST women want before they decide on IT. An "exceptional" woman might just skip all this and cut to the chase, but don't bet on finding this kind of girl too often.

WHAT WOMEN WANT BEFORE THEY DECIDE TO HAVE SEX

ROMANCE

LOTS *Flowers*
OF KISSING
Chivalry

A Statement of Commitment

Little Gifts
and Cards *Flowers*

A statement that tells
them you don't really want   Telling her
them just for their bodies   "I Love You"

(I know, I know)
Flowers

Physical affection everywhere but <u>there</u>

MORE ABOUT THE "F" WORD

I cannot stress this enough. You **have** to warm up on all the other parts of her body before going "further." It's called **FOREPLAY**. And it's definitely for play but it's serious business if you leave it out. "The studies" show most women want <u>at least a half hour of warming up</u> before they feel like having intercourse.

> *There is a point where a woman decides*
> *to make love with a man, and that*
> *point is reached when you have driven*
> *her crazy with desire by <u>not</u> touching*
> *her where she is most sensitive.*

Sometimes, less obvious areas are more sensitive than you would know. How do you figure out which areas they are? Explore first. <u>Listen to the sounds she makes when you touch her</u>. A dead giveaway is a louder sound. Women sometimes even <u>amplify</u> their sounds when you finally find the right spot to indirectly let you know that you're on target. Do not assume that just because EMILY liked ear nibbling that your current love likes it too. Try it, but don't assume. Perhaps it's her feet, or her inner arms. . . .

A Nice Idea Before You Begin

Take her to a lingerie store and tell her that you'd love to see her in a little something. Go into the dressing room with her and ask her to model if you've captured that kind of sweetie. You're going to buy it for her, of course. When you get her home, surprise her with flowers and tell her that she's what you've always dreamed about. This is true, no? . . . For right now you should be thinking <u>yes</u>.

Start By Knowing How To Kiss

Loosen up your mouth! Hard tight kisses are OK, but really good kissers know how to do LOTS of things with their lips. First, brush your teeth! Carry breath mints. Now pay attention to how she kisses. Then do back to her what she's doing to you. She's nuzzling your lower lip? You do the same. Mirror what she is doing. So she's blowing in your ear? That's what she likes, Mike! Try soft brushing, wet ones, and really exploring her mouth with your tongue. How many places can you touch with your mouth without taking her clothes off?

P.S. SOMEONE told me that <u>putting your fingers in her mouth</u> is extremely erotic.

Try "Dry Humping."

This is not about camels, but it may have something to do with De Nial. To be candid, it's pretending to have intercourse but keeping your pants on. Woman become disappointed when you immediately strip to your Calvin's. (Rats, we think, now all the fun's over!) And no, it's not because we're into MAKING YOU BEG. It is because by keeping some material between you and us, we can rub our pubic area against you which feels great! (Psst! The pubic area includes the clitoris, you big gorilla.) After you've simulated intercourse with your clothes on a couple of times, you won't have much trouble going further. In fact, she might remove your shirt and go nuts if you hold out long enough.

Try, "Where would you like me to touch you?" Then continue with, "Like this? Harder? Softer?" Speak in a patient, gentle, and supportive manner. And try to lose your business voice. You are not assembling a car!

Good Foreplay Ideas

(I am always on the lookout for new areas so send me yours and I'll publish it in the next edition.)

Her neck—Open-mouthed biting, not too hard; pretend you're an animal and growl.

Her hair—Tug on it gently; pull it by the nape of the neck. Brushing a woman's hair will drive her wild. It is a nurturing move. It makes her feel taken care of.

Her toes—Suck on them one by one (or massage between the joints.)

Her eyes—Kiss them lightly.

The inside of her arms—A killer for some women; do it lightly!

Her back—Roll her over and kiss from her neck to her tail.

Her arm pit—Bury yourself there. That's her smell.

Her bellybutton—Lick it.

Always a good idea—Breathe, blow on, or gently lick any body part.

Wear her favorite cologne and soft, touchable clothing.

Loosen up your tie—But keep it on as long as possible; remember, it's a power symbol!

Wear great underwear—Avoid the tighty whities. Colors are sexy, however red is amusing; many women like black bikinis. But please, no high riders or g strings unless she's European and that's another book. Boxers aren't as attractive as briefs to most women, but in silk they're sexy. Check out what she likes by trying different styles. Throw away your skivvies with spots, holes or grass stains. Your mother knew best after all.

BEFORE "IT" HAPPENS

Let's get serious for a moment, now. Tell her the good feelings you have about your relationship, and that you want it to continue; this a key point that women need. They are worried that you will leave. Tell her that you respect her boundaries and assure her that you will "wait." Women need to hear that it's OK for them to go slowly. In fact, paradoxically, telling her this may cause her to speed up! When there is no pressure, there is nothing to resist. Aggressive behavior such as pushing yourself on her either physically or verbally will only alienate her. She will feel scared or victimized. A crude or poorly timed comment can completely turn her off. Treat her like a gentle flower, and don't try to play Brando until later.

I strongly suggest, to avoid any misconceptions, that when it appears that you are about to have intercourse you do the following:

Stop and look her in the eyes. Tell her you would really like to make love with her, then ask <u>directly</u> if that's what she wants.

This may give her just the extra incentive she needs to trust you. She wants to feel that she has control over the choice. Many women are not good at saying no. If you persist, she might give in, but resent you for it afterward. Making love to a women who doesn't really want to, <u>who is afraid to say no but gives in</u> may give *you* some temporary physical satisfaction, but *she* may not return for more. And—can you say "date rape" boys and girls? **It is your responsibility to stop, and her responsibility to say no.**

When she says NO she is not testing you. She does <u>not</u> actually means yes. Translation: Lawsuit.

Are there women who say no and later say yes? Of course, but it is a matter of timing. She's <u>coming around</u> to saying yes, but says no in the meantime, and means no when she says it. Again, back off and she'll give way when she's ready.

WHAT WORKS

LONGFOREPLAYLONGFOREPLAYLONGFOREPLAYLONGFOREPLAY

1. Carry her to bed. Carry her whenever you get the chance. It makes you feel big; it makes her feel smaller. Remember this concept. Small equals feeling taken care of.

2. Going slowly in the beginning—passionate and fast at the very end is usually OK if you take time earlier.

3. Whisper stories to her in her primary mode. (See Chapter Eleven— NLP section.) If she is <u>visual</u>, paint her a verbal *picture* about a *beautiful* place. Include lots of colorful adjectives. If she is <u>auditory</u>, tell her to *hear* the *sound* of the water and always pay attention to the tone of your voice. If she is <u>kinesthetic</u>, ask her to imagine the *warmth* of the *sand* between her *toes;* tell her body feels wonderfully *soft.*

4. Call her "baby," "my darlin'," or other endearing names. Experiment. When you're not being sexual, ask her if she likes these words. Names which infer that she is smaller than you unconsciously make her feel protected. Most women will not openly admit that they like these nicknames. We are too nice, politically correct and concerned about the reaction of radical feminism. Women do tell me that if a man calls them "honey," "sweetie," or "doll" before they develop a closer relationship, it is a complete turn-off.

5. Wear cologne. Find out if she likes your brand, then **always use the same one.** Even better, go shopping, ask her to pick out one she likes, then wear it to make sure she really likes it. Scent is a powerful way to get her to remember you. A kinesthetic women may even like the way you smell after you exercise. Ask, if she likes it, then repeat. Women are not as complex as you might think.

6. Listen to the sounds she makes. Try to remember what you were doing when she made them. Do whatever you were doing again. It's her signal.

7. Make love anywhere else but the bed. And don't do it when the kids are in the next room, forcing you to be quiet. Ship them off, rearrange the house for noise control, but find a way to do it with abandon.

8. Women will rarely come right out and say: "I want you to touch me lightly on the insides of my arms, then run your fingers down to the tips of my fingers." If you manage to luck out and actually touch her the way she wants, repeat of course. Again—**Ask, then repeat.** Initially, she will probably be vague, "Oh, I don't know, it all feels good." Women were taught that good girls shouldn't talk about sex. Gently push her to be specific about what she likes sexually. Tell her that you'll tell her what you like if she tells you too. Trade off doing what you each like. A good book for learning how to give each other pleasure is For Each Other by Lonnie Barbach.

9. Lubricants are very helpful. But some uninformed women might get insulted, so ask first. No hand lotion, it causes infections and isn't water soluble with condoms. Use *KY Jelly, Gyne-Moistren, Replens* or other lotions which are water soluble. Astroglide heats up, doesn't stain and tastes sort of sweet. Saliva is fine, but do it discreetly. **Never use oil-based creams, they eat through condoms.** See the end of the chapter.

10. Vibrators. Some women love vibrators and use them to masturbate but will hide them from you. Try referring to them out of bed, and see if she brings it up. Or buy one and experiment! (Surprise her with one that has a bow on it.) If she takes offense, assure her that you were not implying anything, you just thought it would be sexy. Good Vibrations, a store in San Francisco that sells sexual books, toys, and other goodies, has a great assortment in its catalogue.

KEEPING YOUR PASSION ALIVE

Being aroused continuously, especially if you have been together or married a long time, has a lot to do with the newness of a situation—so come up with new and unusual situations and activities to turn her on. Try these:

- **Phone sex:** When you can't be together, phone home.
- **Sexual toys:** See the resource section.
- **Different positions:** And in different places using different aids like chairs, pillows, washing machines, the shower, parked in your front driveway, the floor, the beach, the forest. Or dangerous settings where you could get caught! Like the airplane bathroom which will initiate you into "the mile-high club."

- **Dressing up and acting out roles:** doctor and nurse, fisherman and mermaid, Lola and the devil. Bring costumes, props, the works.

- **Acting out scenarios:** One easy and fun adventure is to act out a scene that involves both of you meeting at a public place and picking each other up as if you had never met.

- **Food:** Try whipped cream, honey, ice cream, even barbecue sauce, strawberries, the works. Those of you who have seen 9 1/2 Weeks surely remember the refrigerator scene with Kim Bassinger?

- **Light changes,** black light, or a different colored light bulb. Oriental love books say that purple is the color of female sexual energy. Any kind of different color is exciting.

- **Blindfolds**

- **Feathers and fur**

- **Silk scarves**

- **Warm wash cloths**

- **Hot water or ice cubes:** Try alternating them during oral sex.

- **Old T-shirts:** Save them and rip them off her.

- **Skin flicks:** Remember that women are interested in movies that show a little buildup and some semblance of a plot rather than just the strip and hump variety that most of these movies offer. Good Vibrations in the resource section has a good list.

- **Going table dancing with her:** Yes, there are some adventuresome women who would enjoy this kind of voyeurism. Women are remarkably curious about "the dark side;" they may like to watch you get turned on. The author confesses to having done this with a significant other (purely as an academic survey, mind you) and things went very well for all concerned.

- **Talking dirty:** Mud! Dustbunnies!
- **Bondage:** Believe it or not, there are some very normal couples who do this kind of thing and never end up on "Hard Copy." Dominance and submission is a fantasy that allows one of the partners to be in control so that the other one is able to let go of their inhibitions more readily. Physical pain is rarely, if ever, inflicted during these playtimes, and authors of several respected clinical sexual books indicate that these kinds of fantasies are very common. So if you're thinking it's perverted—relax. The closer you are to your partner emotionally, the more you will be able to share and experiment with this kind of fantasy.

Note One: No drinking, be careful not to cut off any circulation or use materials that tighten when pulled. Have an "escape" word—when someone says it, the game is over.

"No tying" dominance is the closest you can come to the real thing. Try pinning her hands down with yours, over her head, or at her sides. Try pinning both her hands down with one of yours. The first time this happened to me I thought I was going to die and go to heaven. (The fact that it took place in a car helped immensely.) Just plain sitting on a woman and pinning her hands to the floor or bed will work wonders for the right kind of girl, especially girls that like to get in your face and try to push you around. Try it during <u>sex,</u> my dear, not during a political discussion no matter how much you want to. In fact, maybe if you fantasize about pinning her down when she goes into one of her "speeches," it will be easier to say, "You look sexy when you're mad, come over here and kiss me."

Light bondage with non-hurtful material is sexy to a lot of women. Ask her if she could get into some playful, respectful cowboys and Indians, and that you could act it out by tying each other up. Then, read her facial expression. If she smiles, or at least will discuss it, she probably won't mind if you approach her the right way. This does not mean to jump out of the closet with your handcuffs! Start by using soft scarves. Run them softly over her body, get her in the mood. Tell her she's captured your heart and that you're going to pretend to capture her. You could also suggest that she tie you up first if she felt safer.

Note Two: If she says she doesn't like it <u>stop immediately</u>.

Most women like playful dominance; *but women who have experienced abuse find it scary*. A good idea if your mate starts to freeze up any time during sex is to stop and talk. If she has a hard time getting started, have her get on top of you. It gives her a sense of control.

I strongly suggest that if she exhibits a lot of fear during sex, cries regularly or acts really moody after or during sex that you both seek counseling to find out what's bothering her. <u>It is not just her problem</u>. It should be your concern too.

GETTING ORAL SEX

So if you'd like to know the percentage of women who really like going down on you, or fellatio, as it's clinically called, more than half of all women enjoy doing it. The odds decrease when a woman is over age forty-five. Telling her how important it is to you and perhaps having some couples counseling from a licensed sex therapist may help. There may be some deeper issues going on that are showing themselves in her avoidance. Certainly one possible way to change her mind is to be as giving as you can by pleasing *her* with oral sex. But don't keep track of how often it's happened, and don't try to be manipulative by making her feel guilty. This will turn her off to it even more, and make her think she HAS to do it. If she just doesn't want to do it, I suggest that you live with it and appreciate what you are getting. You have to learn to change your attitude, love her, and accept the way she is.

This issue is one of the reasons that, despite what certain radio therapists are saying, I promote a short period of living together prior to marriage so that both of you can get a clearer picture of what you will be dealing with when and if you do marry. Alcoholism, drug abuse, household habits, sexual proclivities and other fairies both good and not so good fly out of Pandora's box when you shack up. One of my clients found out her guy was an alcoholic within two months, another had a boyfriend who couldn't handle her housekeeping. My rule of thumb is certainly no more than eight months. If you can't tell if you are in love with her by eight months, you either don't love her or you are seriously ambivalent about marriage and commitment. Back to fellatio, here's some other stuff:

- It's pretty common for most guys to have a hard time coming when a woman's mouth is—uh—in direct contact with the penis. It's said that maybe only about half of most guys can.

- It's also pretty common for the girl to gag occasionally. Don't take this personally. The gag reflex is common when something is down your throat.

- You could ask her if she enjoys swallowing. If she doesn't, you can work out some kind of non-verbal signal that tells her when she should pull off.

- Lubricants, chocolate syrup, and other good tasting things can help her to enjoy the experience.

- There are videos that teach some techniques, but the best thing to do it to tell her what you like and where.

GIVING ORAL SEX AND HER ORGASM

Joke: "Why do so many women fake orgasm?"

"Because so many men fake foreplay."

And now, a list of facts you should memorize. Let's get rid of all of those locker room myths and tell the truth. First and foremost, <u>the clitoris is the female sexual organ. It is not the vagina!</u>

More than half of all women need additional stimulation directly to the clitoris to have an orgasm. This means using your hand, a vibrator, or something else to add this additional stimulus.

<u>There is nothing wrong with her if she doesn't come at the drop of a hat.</u> She is not neurotic or frigid; she is absolutely NORMAL. Like you guys, who grew up with the myth that "a real man" can keep it up all night, a lot of women grew up with the myth that "real women" came only through vaginal intercourse, and if they didn't reach orgasm quickly many of them believed there was something wrong with them. This vaginal orgasm myth, which Freud introduced almost one hundred years ago was debunked by Masters and Johnson, the famous sex researchers, back in the mid-1960's. An orgasm originates from the clitoris. Having intercourse causes her clitoris to feel good due to the pulling of skin around it during thrusting, but at best, it is <u>indirect</u> stimulation.

In fact, if you compare the female orgasm to the male orgasm, in terms of "duration," women can certainly sustain THEIR erections for quite a while longer than men can. And yes, the clitoris gets hard when stimulated and swells up. That's because it originated from the same tissue the penis was formed from during fetal development. Women are capable of multiple orgasms, and we like them! Men have a "refractory period" between ejaculations, and they have to rest before going again. (As men age, this period lengthens.)

All women are different. We are capable of becoming aroused by stimulation to all different places in the body, at different times and under different circumstances. So, if you want to be an excellent lover, learn what pleases her. And another thing, please remember that what worked with your last lover will not necessarily work with the next one. Comparing your lovers, if only in your mind can do nothing but harm your relationship. Each woman has different sensations that can get her off, and different wants, needs and fantasies that you should find out about.

You need to tell your lover that it's OK for her to tell you what she wants and where she wants it. But this may be difficult, because again, she wasn't brought up to talk about it. If she is shy, encourage her. Don't just give up and assume that's the way it's going to be and go by guessing.

Oral sex has been found to be the one consistent way that women can reach orgasm. Some of the suggestions from the authors of *Men's Health* magazine included alternating temperatures of hot and cold on the clitoral area using hot tea and cool water, spelling out the alphabet with the tongue (try not to hum the tune that goes with it), using two fingers in the vagina while stimulating the clitoris with the tongue or other fingers, and finding and stimulating the "G" spot. Stimulating the nipples while the clitoris is touched is a good idea too.

When women masturbate, they come just as quickly as men do, for they know exactly where and how hard to touch themselves. Of course it takes you longer to help her come because it's not your body! So learn and ask, and get rid of your old stereotypes.

THE "G" SPOT AND OTHER GOOD AREAS

The "G" spot is an area located behind the front upper wall of the vaginal opening. If you reach in with your finger and hook it toward the front of her body or her pubic bone you will locate it. This is an area that has a lot of nerve endings, and many women get a lot of intense pleasure when it is stimulated. This nerve plexus swells to the size of a dime or larger.

In most women, the deep interior walls of the vagina don't have much sensation; however, the first two inches of the vagina's entrance does. The folds of flesh, or lips of the vagina which surround the opening are very sensitive; these are called the labia minora. The labia majora, the longer, outer lips are less sensitive.

Did you know there's a neural connection between a woman's breasts, nipples, and vagina, and sometimes stimulating her vaginal area can cause sensations there as well? Did you also know that stimulating other parts of her body can cause her to have erotic feelings in her mouth? The mouth and the genitals have the largest supply of nerve endings so it makes sense that getting these two parts together will make beautiful mouth music. And as long as you don't hum the alphabet, the vibration of your lips can create a very nice feeling.

Note: Don't blow into her vagina! It can cause an air bubble to enter her bloodstream which could be fatal, especially if she's pregnant.

OK. Some guys don't like giving a woman oral sex because of the odors. Well, guess what, your penises are not exactly rose gardens, either. So take a bath together first, and use scented, edible lubricants, food or whipped cream.

PROBLEMS

Erection Problems

If you are experiencing problems with erections, read *Male Sexuality* by Bernie Zilbergeld, listed in the reference section. It will really help you. Written from a male point of view by a male doctor, it should be required reading for all men and women. In most cases, problems with erections can be eliminated through simple behavioral exercises that are taught in this book. Practice masturbating with a lighter touch, using the "stop-start," or "the squeeze" technique.

Health

I will pass on some advice about something that you should be doing all along. The reason a great majority of men are having erectile problems is that they are sick. **Impotence is directly related to age and physical health**. If you take care of your body, you are far more likely to be giving all those widows out there a happy retirement.

■ **Eat leaner foods.** The arteries that supply the blood to Mr. Happy for his erection get clogged or narrowed by cholesterol deposits. In fact, most of the problems connected with erections have everything to do with blood flow. If you exercise, you will raise the good ratio of LDL/ HDL.

■ **Stop smoking!** The probability that you will have erectile problems is more than double if you smoke.

■ **Stop drinking!** And, did you know that alcohol is a depressant? It has a numbing effect on the nervous system. Feeling no pain equals no sexual gain.

---

70 to 80 percent of males who are alcoholics have decreased sexual drive or erection problems.

■ **Investigate the medicine you are taking.** Some meds definitely decrease sexual drive. By the way, Trazodone, a drug used to treat depression, has actually been known to <u>help</u> men with their erections.

■ **Get some rest** and go on vacation. With less stress you won't be tense and so worried about "performance." You are not a trained seal!

There are three new promising drugs that will hopefully be soon be approved for helping impotence. *Viagra*, by *Pfizer, Inc.* has been shown to be eighty percent effective with impotence, and as of the print date, it may be available by April of 1998! The chemical name is for Viagra is *Sildenafil*. *Apomorphine* has been shown to be seventy percent effective with psychological impotence, and is made by *Tap Pharmaceuticals Inc.* The FDA may approve it before 1999 due to promising studies. *Vasomax* is an oral version of a current injection drug that dilates penile blood vessels. It will be produced by *Zonagen Inc.* and may be approved by the end of 1997.

Here are Some Indicators That Your Problem May Be Emotional:

1. You can get an erection with one partner, but not the other. The fact that you may have two partners to begin with might be the problem. Especially if you are struggling with your morality.

2. You are going through serious stress, for example, a divorce or job problems.

3. You have a history of depression or other mental illness.

4. You don't have an obvious medical problem like diabetes or heart disease.

Testosterone

If you feel as if your sex drive has driven off without you, there may be a simple explanation: If you are over fifty, your testosterone level starts to drop. Doctors are now considering testosterone augmentation treatment, see them for details.

Your penis is connected to your heart, (remember you need all that blood?) There's a very BIG possibility that your penis knows something you don't know and is trying to tell you something. Mr. Happy's unhappiness is what you need to figure out. Anxiety comes with lots of symptoms, and Mr. Happy's poor spirits may be one of them.

So why are you unhappy? Perhaps, as famous sex therapists say, you are watching yourself and your "performance" rather than participating in the pleasure of it. You are worrying too much about her and not focusing on your own pleasure.

And you can't be a good lover to her if you aren't feeling anything. "Sensate focus" exercises, which are discussed in *Male Sexuality,* are a good place to start. These exercises are good for both men and women. Plus, there is an extra benefit to slowing down and taking more time for yourself— SHE likes it when you go slower! Take the pressure off and hold and kiss each other. Just enjoy each other's bodies without thinking there is some kind of "goal line," (her orgasm, my erection); the rest will come naturally, in time. *For Each Other* by Lonnie Barbach is an excellent book that contains couples exercises for mutual pleasure.

Premature Ejaculation

In my lectures I like to say jokingly that "premature" is defined as anything less than an hour. But given the number of serious faces I see, I know that the topic is not fun. In reality many men who aren't sexually experienced, or men who have gone long periods without it usually come rapidly. This is a very <u>normal</u> situation. But how to improve it? There's the *squeeze technique* where you or you together with your partner stimulate yourself until you feel the urge, then squeeze three to four seconds with the thumb under the penis below the head. After the urge to come goes away, start up again, and then repeat. You can also try the *stop-start* method. Go as long as you can, then pull out and let your erection subside. The more you practice this, the more you'll build up tolerance and have longer intercourse. Or you can practice masturbating alone, stop when you feel you have to come, and gradually work up to longer and longer periods of erections.

I mention the woman being involved with the process because you are both in this together. If she's an understanding lover, she will gladly help you out. Talk with her about it. Remember that YOU ARE SENSITIVE AND THIS IS GOOD! That's much better than being shut down to your feelings.

Inability to Ejaculate

Some men have difficulty reaching orgasm at all despite a patient partner and relaxing situations. Of course, this is true for women as well. Doctors believe that there is underlying rage at women, anger toward parents, or other psychological problems that are interfering with the ability to trust, for orgasm certainly requires letting go. Some men were sexually abused as children, and this interferes. Certainly if the guy is guilty about an extracurricular affair, this could be the problem. First, rule out any medical issues, and then see a good licensed sex therapist.

A LIST OF WHAT DOESN'T WORK

The follow sexual situations have bothered women quite a bit. We thought you might like to know so you would knock this stuff off.

1. The old "You've gotten me so turned on, and now I have to go home like this? Do you know how hard this (it) is?" Guilt just isn't sexy.

2. "Would you like me to rub your back?"

3. "What are you, frigid?" (No, just around jerks, thank God.)

4. Refusing to wear a condom because <u>you</u> don't run around with drug addicts!

5. Asking a woman if she climaxes easily before having any sexual contact, or talking about intimate sexual details when you barely know her. This is not erotic, nor does it get her in the mood. It is intrusive and immature.

6. Asking a woman to take a shower first (alone) before you have oral sex with her. How would you feel if she jumped up and washed out her mouth after having oral sex with you? If cleanliness is important, arrange to take a shower or bath <u>together</u> first.

7. <u>Guaranteed to turn her off</u>: Touch her breasts or vagina as soon as you can. Or, say to her "I'm waiting for you to come first" as you hold back your orgasm, before understanding how she has hers. Another reason why some women fake it.

8. <u>Sticking your tongue in her mouth the first time you kiss her</u>. All right, I confess to this one. The first <u>four</u> count 'em, FOUR boys who kissed me in high school decided on this less than sexy ap-

proach. I think they all read the same *Mad* magazine. I suppose I've been peeved by this ever since. As ever, to avoid bias, I decided to check out whether this was just some freak occurrence that only *I* was cursed with. Miracle of miracles, every woman in all of my women's classes agreed with me. (All but one <u>exceptional</u> woman who said if she REALLY liked him it wouldn't matter, but she was European so does that count?) I suggest you ask your "platonic" female friends what they think. Let her make the first move with her tongue; that will let you know when she is ready.

9. If you smoke and she doesn't, it is nearly impossible not to taste the tobacco on your breath, or smell the smoke on your clothes. It is a turn-off to nearly all non-smokers.

10. Coming quickly, then doing nothing to give us pleasure. Let the woman have her orgasm first, this usually helps. It actually is a physiological fact that men want to go to sleep afterward, but women don't know this so we get upset when you do.

11. Finishing and then not talking at all afterward— even a little bit. You don't have to engage in a lengthy discussion, just tell her you loved making love to her, and that you like feeling close. Fight your urge to bolt by *communicating*—a rare occurrence after sex with most men.

12. Fighting in bed. You will begin to associate bed as the place where serious problems happen. This is not sexy. Get up and fight in the garage. *Keep your negative feelings out of the bedroom.*

13. Contortionist sexual positions are great for some women, but some have bad backs, or are just plain embarrassed by what you suggest. Let her warm up to your new positions. Sneak into them slowly. Reading books on sex <u>together</u> can clarify what she likes and doesn't like. Buy books that

show sexual positions and share them with her. Leave them on the night stand, and then see if she'll talk about it.

14. Having sex* with her for the first time, and then not calling her the next day. Most women are now refraining from having intercourse until they know the man better. No doubt, you probably have already noticed this. The sixties and seventies are dead, you old dudes. Just be glad that you went through that glorious era and didn't have to worry about condoms and AIDS! If the woman has a sense of her personal limits, she has been thinking about sex quite a bit before she decides to do it. When she *does* decide to have sex with you, if you disappear the next day, I cannot be held responsible for the warfare.

Want to know just how she felt about your lovemaking? Pay attention to how she acts right afterward or in the morning if you made love the night before. What does she say and, more importantly, HOW does she say it? If she is quiet or withdrawn, or on the other hand acts bitchy or demanding (which is a psychological cover for being hurt) chances are she didn't really want to do it or that you were a less than sensitive lover.

Remember, though, that she did make a choice by not saying no. You are not responsible for her ambivalence. You *are* responsible for rude, insensitive lovemaking. <u>Getting a statement that yes, she wants to have sex makes her decision very clear.</u> Isn't the point of all this to get some regular, <u>repeat</u> affection? Don't blow it after you've gotten this far by acting like a jerk.

*An important note: "Sex" to a woman means touching her vagina and/or her breasts. *Sexual contact does not have to be intercourse for it to feel like sex to her.*

ABOUT DISEASE

Question: How do people get infected?

Answer: By having sex with people they think are not infected.

Below is a list of activities that can expose you to HIV. The only way you can get HIV is through intimate contact with infected body fluids:

Blood, semen, vaginal secretions, and rarely, saliva.

1. Unprotected sex—or sex without a latex condom.

- Do not use natural skin condoms; they allow the virus to pass through.
- Use lots of water-based lubricant to avoid condom breakage. K-Y Jelly, spermicidal cream, Astroglide, or saliva.
- Oil-based lubricants DO NOT WORK and cause the condom to fall apart: Do not use petroleum jelly, cold cream, hand lotion, baby oil, Monistat, Vagisil.
- Use a spermicide that kills HIV.
- Other kinds of birth control methods don't protect against the virus: the pill, the sponge, IUDs, diaphragms.

2. Anal sex, which can cause abrasions lets the virus pass through.

3. Oral sex on a woman without using "a dental dam," which is a sheet of latex that dentists use laid over the vagina. Oral sex is especially dangerous when she is having her period. You can order the Kia-Ora Lollyes dam through the *Blowfish* catalogue, see the reference section.

4. Oral sex on a man without a condom. If you have open cuts in your mouth your risk is greatly increased.

5. Semen in mouth.

6. Oral-anal contact without using a dental dam.

7. Sharing sexual aids.

8. Blood contact of any kind including menstrual blood.

9. Sharing needles, anything that can cause bleeding.

10. Unprotected sex with multiple partners. Especially people who are high risk, drug users or prostitutes.

11. STDs that cause sores on the skin—herpes or gonorrhea. The sores open a pathway into the bloodstream.

12. Sports. If blood is splashed during injury and gets into open cuts, or on mucous membranes.

13. HIV in small amounts can be in the saliva. The virus can pass by wet kissing if either partner has open sores or cuts in the mouth.

Most people develop HIV within 2 to 12 weeks after being exposed. However, it can take as long as six months. To be sure, wait at least six months after the event that may have exposed you, and get an HIV test.

New developments as of 1997: Protease inhibitors are drugs that interrupt the viral cycle of HIV. These are new drugs that keep the virus from reproducing, but they don't prevent HIV transmission: Names of two of these drugs are *Saquinavir* (or Invirase) and *Viracept*

Herpes

Information courtesy of Haines Ely, MD. Dermatologist:

Herpes has taken a back seat in the HIV paranoia wagon. It used to be "the gift that keeps on giving," everyone's greatest sexual fear. In the 1970's it made the front cover of Time and Newsweek. Men and women entering a new relationship may feel confident they don't have HIV, especially if they have had a blood test. Some people married and monogamous since before 1980 (when AIDS first appeared) don't even bother to have themselves tested. Herpes doesn't even enter the thought process until one of the sexual partners becomes infected.

There are at least eight known herpes virus types. The two which concern us are herpes simplex virus type 1 which causes the familiar "cold sore" or "fever blister" on the lips and type 2 which usually infects the genitals. Between 25 and 40% of genital herpes is HSV 1, resulting from oral sex. Genital herpes infections increased 16-fold between 1966 and 1984. Since 1984 there has been a 31% increase in the prevalence of herpes simplex virus type 2. Let's take the course of genital herpes step by step:

A primary genital herpes infection occurs in a patient seronegative for antibodies to both HSV 1 and 2. This means that a blood test for an immune response (antibodies) to the virus is negative. If the test were positive the person has already had herpes and this isn't the first episode. The virus gets into the skin and travels to the regional lymph nodes and local nerves. There is a systemic reaction to the first episode which may be quite severe. There may be fever, headache, and muscle pains which precede the skin eruption by several days. The skin lesions begin as redness, with soreness or stinging and itching sensations, followed by crops of little blisters which may be all grouped together in a bunch. The blisters may be on several parts of the external genitals, in the pubic hairy area, or in the vagina. The blisters and symptoms may last up to three weeks. After resolution of the skin lesions the virus becomes latent in the regional nerve ganglion for life. This means that there is no visible virus present, but the virus DNA is encoded in the nucleus of nerve cells, usually in the sacral ganglion. The pudendal nerve, which enervates the penis in men, and the external genitalia in women, also has a branch which enervates the buttocks in women. This nerve is connected directly to the sacral ganglion.

Recurrent episodes of genital herpes are common after the initial infection. The recurrences mimic the initial episode, but now the person has antibodies to the virus and the episodes and symptoms are less severe. The antibodies can't "see" or kill the virus while it is latent in nerve cells so even though antibodies are present the body never gets rid of the virus.

A recurrence of skin blistering occurs when the virus travels from the nerve to the skin. There is a "prodrome" of symptoms before blisters appear. There is usually a flu-like syndrome of low fever, ill-feeling, headache, and almost always emotional storms. It has often been said that herpes simplex flares after a severe emotional upset. The emotional upset itself is often a symptom that the virus has been activated, rather than a cause. It is part of the prodrome. Itching, tingling, or pain in the skin precedes the blistering eruption by several hours to several days. The blisters, once they appear, are absolutely loaded with virus and are highly contagious.

The blisters crust and scab and resolve over a period of five to ten days. This pattern may repeat itself every three weeks, for years, or may gradually taper off to one attack per year. The average is four per year, for life. However, viral shedding may occur in asymptomatic carriers of herpes simplex up to 4% of the days between episodes. This means that once one has had herpes there is the possibility of infecting some one who hasn't had it, even if no blisters are present and one hasn't had an active episode for months.

Remember the pudendal nerve branch which goes to the buttocks in women? Many women have recurrent herpetic infection of the buttock. It appears as a little itchy spot and may not ever be diagnosed as herpes. However, the victim is highly contagious when it is present, especially when sleeping in the "spooning" position with a partner. If all this isn't bad enough, one can get a second infection of herpes from the type one didn't get the first time. A high antibody titer to type 1 may not protect from a new infection with type 2. There is also much higher infection rate of HIV in persons who have genital herpes. This is probably because the open sores left by the blisters are an easy portal of entry for HIV virus.

Herpes can easily make one a sexual cripple. Safe sex, and honest inquiry of your partner's history before entering a sexual relationship are the best techniques for avoidance.

Fortunately there is effective treatment (but not cure) by prescription from an M.D. Acyclovir (Zovirax) has been the treatment of choice for the past twelve years. It is poorly absorbed, but quite effective. More recently valacyclovir (Valtrex) has come on the market. It is converted to acyclovir in the body and gives much higher blood levels. Famcyclovir is a similar drug and is undergoing trials for treatment of genital herpes. There are no creams or lotions which have a significant effect on the disease (since the virus lives in the nerves). For those who have few episodes of genital herpes, beginning Valtrex at the first hint of prodromal symptoms can often stop or significantly shorten an attack. For those who have frequent recurrences, taking one tablet a day often keeps the herpes away. Studies of patients taking daily acyclovir for years have attested to the remarkable safety of this drug.

L-lysine is a popular folk remedy for herpes infections. The theory behind its use is that lysine competes with argenine (another amino acid) in the structure of the herpes virus cell wall. Too much lysine competes with argenine so that the virus can't replicate itself. Unfortunately argenine is prevalent in chocolate and nuts, two foods which attract lonely hearts. Red wine, and grape skins have also been shown to have a preventative effect against herpes virus infections. Welch's grape juice will do if one doesn't eat grapes or drink red wine daily. The gold standard of therapy is still acyclovir. Lysine or grape products may make one feel better but I wouldn't rely on them if I had herpes. The bottom line is: don't catch herpes if you can avoid it!

WHY WOMEN GET EMOTIONAL AFTER SEX

Women feel ambivalent about sex. You probably already figured that out. We have much more at stake than you do.

We could get pregnant!

We might choose to have an abortion!

You could leave us!

After sex, men have coyote mornings and women want to buy silver sets.

Sex means more and has more consequences for a woman than it initially does for a man. While you may merely be interested in getting laid, we have made an *emotional* commitment to you. We want to be sure that you are interested in us before we let you get close and we have no assurances that you will stick around afterward. It's a dangerous game we play. That is why we wait so long to decide; we look for clues and signs of your love and commitment. It has been said that a man will tell a woman, "I'm not just telling you I love you to get you into bed," in order to do just that. But the smart women, who is aware of these games, will not let herself to get in bed with you until she's sure you are sincere. <u>Expect her to withdraw if you don't make emotional contact with her after sex.</u> *You must assure her you are not going to leave and that you care about her if you want the sex to continue.*

Female wiring causes an unconscious urge to build a nest after sex. This is why women WANT TO GET SERIOUS after they sleep with you, even though the night before they might have just wanted TO DO IT, and nothing more (or so we tell ourselves). Despite our urge to be independent and our political position to keep our sexuality as free as we are, biology urges most women to choose one mate and settle down. <u>A decision to have sex with you is an unconscious decision to choose you as a mate.</u>

A woman who makes you wait has some standards:

1. She doesn't want to die.
2. She hopes to avoid getting hurt by waiting.
3. She's picky and probably not sleeping around—be glad she made you wait!

When I finally figured out what most men had on their minds, I began saving myself a lot of grief by delaying sex. The men who clearly had no other intentions but scoring disappeared rapidly. The men who wanted to get to know me and have an emotional connection as well as a physical one stayed around. It was those men I decided to get sexually involved with. It was an easy barometer.

Remember gentlemen, the best sex you will experience is that of body and of the spirit. *The spirit of a woman moves through her emotional center, which is her heart.* If you can learn to understand how she feels, if you will be supportive and assertive, if you can learn to be a sensitive and compassionate lover, you will be on your way to heaven.

Now is that too much too ask?

"There are two types of women: Those who wear well and those who wear little."

—*Walter Steightiff*

"Bait the hook
    well. This fish
will bite."

—*Shakespeare*

Universal **11**
Attraction
Tactics

All right, let's get something straight before you read this chapter. On occasion I been accused of teaching men and women to be—manipulative. Consider this, guys; isn't it <u>dishonest</u> to wear a nice suit to work to impress your boss so you can get a raise when you really feel like working in different clothes. . . aren't you being manipulative? Better you should schlep in wearing your old ketchup-stained sweatshirt? No, it's just <u>smart</u> to look sharp. If you want a promotion, you practice goal-oriented behavior to get it. Isn't it <u>manipulative</u> to take a bath so you don't smell? Better you should be yourself and let her appreciate your natural aroma? Right. You think that she should be able to accept little old you for exactly the way you are? And what if <u>she</u> is promiscuous and likes to run around with other guys? Surely you should be able to accept that too if you're an OPEN CARING GUY who appreciates women for the way that they really are. . . And I suppose that Michael Jordan was simply born with the ability to make great shots and so he didn't have to practice?

OK. I've got a way for you to look at this chapter that will be easier for you to swallow. We humans have these habits called psychological defenses. They are there so we don't get hurt. Think of the defense system like a fortress wall protecting the heart of the girl you want. If you try the direct way in, the soldier that's guarding the heart inside will call out "Hey, somebody wants in RIGHT NOW'. . .Red Alert!".
. . The order comes to fight you off because the last time she let someone in, there was this BIG WOODEN HORSE, see, that he sent as a gift first. . . . Maybe you are THE REAL THING but she doesn't know it yet, so she prepares for the worst. Boiling oil? The cold shoulder? A bitchy attitude?And so, I suggest that you think about the techniques I offer in this chapter as ladders to get over the fortress wall of her defense system, tools to disarm the burglar alarms and calm the sentries, gifts to soothe her savage and wounded soul, shortcuts to learn how to get to her superb hardwiring, <u>the best software that will run on her system to get the results that you want</u>. Let's begin.

INTERMITTENT REINFORCEMENT

In the arsenal of influence that you will use to storm her fortress walls, this technique is perhaps the most powerful. Thousands of studies have taught us that not always responding to the person we want to attract will result in longer, and greater affection from that person. Responding to them intermittently, or off and on will cause them to be uncertain of you. If you use this technique the woman you are attracted to will:

- Work harder to earn your affection and
- Be <u>more</u> attracted to you for a <u>longer</u> period of time.

<u>Never</u> rewarding the behavior of the person you want to attract will eventually cause that person to lose interest. <u>Always</u> rewarding the behavior like the doormat often does will cause your target to become lazy. She may think, "Why

is he so eager? He barely knows me. He'll always be around, so I don't have to work very hard to please him." This is <u>not</u> the way you want her to think about you.

This is why the jerk scores with intermittent reinforcement, although he usually doesn't know that he is using it. He comes and goes when he wants, in a random fashion, activating the trigger of **now you have him, now you don't.** Just when the girl thinks she's over him, he shows up again, and she's hooked.

This is also why relationships burn themselves out when you go too fast, too soon. She feels smothered by your affection, overwhelmed with the constant attack on the walls of her defense. Psychologically, she can only take in so much at a time. She knows too much about you, and hasn't had sufficient time to integrate the information that she does have. And if you've been giving her "the rush," she has entirely too much information to begin with. Like a sponge, she can only soak up so much information at a time. So give her some space to dry out in between times, go slower, avoid wearing out your welcome; don't always give women what they want. Breaking a date now and then or appearing unpredictable activates the off and on trigger.

This does not mean acting unkind, or abusive.

It just means that you will not <u>always</u> be available to her; you will create uncertainty, an element of doubt in her mind. Will he or won't he? Does he or doesn't he? Because we are animals, we want the thrill of the chase, so let <u>her</u> chase <u>you</u> a bit, you are worth it—aren't you? If you fear losing her because you let some time elapse between dates, you've got it all wrong. You will lose her if you <u>don't</u> give her breathing room! You must value yourself enough to have other women you are dating while she solidifies her feelings about you. Remember, keep three eggs in your basket, and avoid suffocating her. If she thinks she can control you, she will not be excited by you. Why should we work to have more when we have already had it all? We get bored if we don't have to work for what we want and we move on to other, more challenging offers. Intermittent reinforcement creates excitement. Passion is out of control . . .

Passion is unpredictable

THE SCARCITY PRINCIPLE

The human tendency to value what we don't always have available to us has been called the principle of scarcity. What is harder to attain appears to be more valuable to us. If we have to work harder to get someone's complete attention, we want to justify the effort we have already put into the relationship by continuing to want what we have worked for—this is known as **the consistency principle**. Absence does truly make the heart grow fonder. It allows her to fantasize about you, to wonder what you are doing. So, *you* be the first to get off the phone, to get out of bed after sex, to have other things to do besides hang around with her for hours on end. Your interest in your own activities, in putting yourself first makes you look desirable, and it makes her miss you.

Other ways to make the scarcity principle work for you is to actually be scarce. Fill up your calendar with things to do and places to be. Shy men often have no other social activities they are involved in. Besides work, the internet, or the TV they have very little contact with women, and so, they appear introverted, quiet, or conversely needy or desperate when they do get around them. Women are attracted to men who are movers and shakers, men who have a lot going on in their lives and who have other women that want their attention. The more activities you are involved with the more socializing you will do and the better your people skills will be.

Another way to use the scarcity principal is to have a great time with her, then lay low, or go on a long trip. She'll have lots of time to fantasize about what you may be doing with other women and when you come back she'll be happy and eager to see you.

THE CONSISTENCY PRINCIPLE

Our tendency to want to appear consistent is used the world over by salespeople. Also called the foot-in-the-door technique, once we have made a commitment to another person, another product, an appointment, an agreement, no matter how small, it is very difficult to avoid coming back for more. We want to appear consistent, responsible and rational in our behavior. That's why consistent coffee dates or minor league contact with the woman you want *now and then* at the beginning (activating intermittent reinforcement) can lead to bigger things. Be consistently interested in the girl you want to attract, always show them that you are glad to see her, but don't be overly available and remember use to use intermittent reinforcement. Here is an example of how powerful our tendency to be consistent is. Many of my divorced clients tell me they knew just before their wedding that they didn't want to go through with it, but <u>convinced themselves that they really did</u> in order to appear consistent. That's why getting someone to agree to a minor request is the first step toward a much larger one. In fact, if your lover has left you, you have a good chance of getting her back if you mend your ways, because she is used to you, has already felt affection for you, and invested much time and energy in your relationship. Her urge to appear consistent may pull you back together as I discuss at the end of this chapter.

So, what you need to do is to try to get her to spend as much time on a regular basis with you as possible. This doesn't have to be romantic time, it can be work time or project time. The more energy she puts into being with you, the more likely she is to view the time you spend together as a relationship, and the more likely she is to want to go out with you when you make a romantic move. And later on, the more likely she is to view the relationship as an asset which she doesn't want to lose.

This is one of the reasons that men don't want to leave their wives despite the fact that they have fallen out of love. Think of all the time and years invested, the material possessions, the verbal commitments, and especially the written agreement of the marriage vow or the business agreement. To break away from his wife means that he will have to break all of these overt and covert agreements. And the stronger that these ties are in terms of time and cash, the more difficult it will be to break away.

One of the ways that certain "experts" in the field of matrimony teach women to get men to commit to them (although I don't condone this) is to tell them to try to get the man to buy them things, expensive things in particular. The more the man spends on her, the more likely he is to view their relationship as an investment. And it is certainly wise to hang on to an expensive investment, isn't it? This is a direct use of the consistency principle to invoke a plausible reason to marry.

So the plan here is to get her to invest time and energy in being with you, and to try to position yourself as an important, integral part of her life that she doesn't want to lose. The more tangible connections that she has with you, the more likely she is to transfer her romantic affections to you as well. Link business with pleasure as much as possible. If she doesn't choose you, does she lose her business prospects as well? This principle carried to an unethical extreme becomes very dirty and underhanded, and has also formed the grounds for many a sexual harassment case.

THE FAVOR

This influence technique is among the most powerful techniques available to us. It is the basis for building civilizations and getting along with others. Long before the coin of the realm, we bartered services to distribute our workload.

"To owe someone" is not pleasant, and we will do anything we can to avoid being in someone's debt. Consider the power of buying a woman a drink, an expensive dinner, two tickets to the opera. Or the power of a great home-cooked meal, or fantastic sex. We want to reciprocate. By putting another in our debt, we have a great advantage. This is why women are not allowing men to pay for them so often, they don't want to feel obliged so it's easier to say no. Imagine how difficult it would be for a woman to go away on a vacation, have the man pay for it, and not feel that she somehow had to pay him back. The rest is left up to your imagination. Flowers create the same urge to reciprocate with kindness. "First time's free?" Not exactly.

I once asked a handsome man to have dessert with me after meeting him at our health club. Because I asked, I insisted on paying the check. Clearly, he didn't want to continue the relationship, but what was interesting was his uneasiness with the situation. After dessert, on the way to the parking lot, he felt so uncomfortable that *he gave me a golf hat* from his car to relieve his natural urge to repay me.

What about getting a woman pregnant, whether you wanted to or not. Because of her inconvenience in carrying the child, and your biologic wiring to protect the mother of your child, you have to pay—the courts, at the very least. Many a husband has allowed himself to be roped into staying with his wife because she "suddenly" became pregnant; the power of the consistency rule is also operating here. However, you both exchange favors; you do her the favor of giving her your sperm; she carries the child and <u>usually</u> does most of the parenting should you split up. Why else would sperm bank donors, egg donors and "host mothers" get paid for their services? If you don't think carrying a child is a big favor, try carrying a sack of fifteen-pound rocks on your body for nine months, and risking death to do it. Why else would a husband stay with a newly pregnant wife or girlfriend he didn't love if not out of obligation to her, society or God? Obligation means returning the favor.

Utilize the power of the favor, but make sure that she *does* reciprocate. If you are doing all the giving, and she doesn't repay you somehow, she will resent you for putting her in your debt, and you will look like a doormat. Or, she might accept your gifts but reciprocate in ways that set you up to be "the friend." For, if she isn't interested in you romantically, she won't reciprocate with physical affection. Make sure you get paid back, or activate intermittent reinforcement and *don't always do her the favor*. She will appreciate it more if she gets it less, therefore she will be more likely to act on her feelings of obligation.

NLP—PREDICATE, SENSORY AND LIFESTYLE MATCHING

NLP, or *Neuro-Linguistic Programming* is a set of physical and verbal behaviors that can indirectly cause others to be more receptive to us. This is done through matching grammatical predicates or verbs, body language, verbal pacing as well as personal habits. Helping someone to be receptive to us means that we learn to speak in their sensory mode, and do things with them that they most like to do.

Each person gets into their inner world through three main sense channels: **visual, auditory**, or **kinesthetic**. By matching a person's given mode, it is possible to indirectly influence that person's tendency to feel closer to you.

First, figure out which sense the person you are interested in usually uses. Ask open-ended questions about their past such as "Tell me about San Francisco." Then watch which direction their eyes go in, and listen for the verbs they use. Don't ask them, "What did San Francisco <u>look</u> like when you were young," because they will answer visually, even if they may be an auditory or a kinesthetic.

Also, gather clues from their lifestyles—a pattern will soon become evident. You need to understand what triggers each type of person. You should also know which sensory type you are as well. If both of you are of the same type, you will feel naturally in sync. If you have different modes, you may frequently feel like you aren't on the same <u>wavelength</u> (that's an auditory description) or that <u>you aren't seeing eye to eye</u> (a visual description) or that <u>something feels off</u> (a kinesthetic description). Practice understanding the world through her eyes. It would be a serious mistake to dismiss or criticize her desires and habits because <u>you</u> don't like or agree with them. Her habits and desires are an integral part of the way she experiences her world.

Many people have a primary and a secondary mode, but with a little investigation, one will stand out more than the other. A very small percentage of us are equally balanced in all modes; that is, we feel, listen, <u>and</u> picture things in our mind using each sense about the same amount of time. We also <u>talk</u> to others in the same language that we think about things, and have lifestyles which reflect this language.

The Visual

A person who represents their internal world **visually** will use visual words such as, "I get a <u>picture</u> of what you're saying," "I <u>see</u>," or "I can <u>imagine</u>." Other visual words:

bright	focus
color	view
clear	illuminate
flash	perspective

Visuals are orderly and neat. Their houses are clean, and they have interesting art on their walls, arranged for a certain effect. They like taking pictures and they like picture books. It is important to pay attention to the way you dress if you want to attract a visual. Primary visuals will always look you over first when they go out with you. They are stimulated by what they see you wearing when they go out with you. Remember what you are wearing and what they comment on, that's the shirt or coat they like, and they'll probably remember the color as well. Go places which have beautiful views and are visually stimulating like museums or aquariums. On long drives, let them look out the window. Park and look at the sunset and go to movies as much as you can!. Rent videos. Visuals often talk rapidly, or gesture a lot with their hands. They tend to be active and outgoing. Their breathing is often rapid and shallow and from the upper chest.

When they think, their eyes go up to the left or right, or gaze straight out in the distance. They are *seeing* their memories. When you ask them where they were brought up, watch which direction their eyes go and what words they choose. If she speaks primarily in visual words and her eyes go up to the left or right, she's probably a visual.

Visuals are impressed with what they see. They like concrete gifts that are pretty and unique that they can place on the table and LOOK at. Take pictures of the two of you together and give them to her, it's one of the best gifts you can give her. Make sure you always look immaculate. Never leave your house or your car messy, and remember to speak in visual words when you are making love with her: "You can SEE how I feel about you," or "You LOOK as pretty as a PICTURE," or "I can't IMAGINE how I'm going to go through the week without you."

The visual woman is the most "high-maintenance" woman of the three types. If you fall for one, you must remember that she will not be happy without things that are pretty around her and a world which is orderly and neat. She's not going to want to grub around and go hiking on the weekends with you (that's what a kinesthetic wants to do); she wants to be visually stimulated and be places where she can SEE things that she likes.

The Auditory

People with an **auditory** internal representation system would be likely use phrases such as "I <u>hear</u> you," "<u>listen</u> to that," or "that <u>sounds</u> good to me." They love to listen as well as talk. They have an incredible ability to concentrate on sound. They are <u>tuned in</u> to animals and like to <u>talk</u> to them. A dead giveaway is a woman with a fantastic set of CDs. I find that most women are usually kinesthetic or visual, so if you see this kind of audio equipment at her house you have a very strong hint that she may be an auditory. (As a whole, men are more auditory than women.)

Auditory women have increased sensitivity to sound, and dislike noise, particularly harsh sounds. One question I ask in my seminars is how would they react if they had to drive an hour's distance to the nearest town and the CD player or radio in their car was broken. The auditories in the room immediately shake their head and look distressed. **An auditory would not be caught dead without the radio or music on.** Especially during love making. Sometimes they leave the TV on for background noise.

Be aware of the sound level wherever you take an auditory. Make sure it is pleasant and melodious; for example, avoid traffic sounds. Go to concerts, have long talks on the phone, or give gifts of sound to her in order to attract her. Try wind chimes or a great CD. **Always have music on when you are with her, and of course learn the kind she likes.** Whisper in her ear and use sensual sounds freely. Auditory people may sit in the "listening position," hand to the side of the head, with their head tilted, as if "listening." **Their eyes move horizontally when they are remembering something,** and they may exhale or sigh when they remember. Their breathing, which is usually regular, will be even more regular as they tell you about conversations with friends, the sound of the birds chirping on the tenth hole of golf, and how it was so quiet you could hear the ball ZING through the air. They might point to their ear when they are talking with you, or cup their hands in back of their ears. Some auditory signal words are:

hear	rings a bell
tune in	buzz
be heard	sound
loud	deaf
tell	saying

The Kinesthetic

The **kinesthetic** might say, "I get a grip on what you're say-ing," "I sense that it's the right thing to do," or "That doesn't feel right. **They are *feelers*, and experience their world through body movement, and through their internal emotional feelings about the world around them.** They want their world to be *comfortable* and they might be disor-ganized or messy. Words that a kinesthetic might use:

sense	get a grip
feel	grab
you know	warm
cold	fits
gut feeling	touched

The way a kinesthetic's world appears is less important than how they feel about it. **More introverted than others, they may also talk less frequently or slowly, and look down or inward when they remember something.** They like to be outside and close to nature. They are relatively low main-tenance, except for the fact that they tend to be messy and as such, will drive a visual person bananas because they don't close cupboards, tend to leave dishes in the sink, clothes on the floor, and books scattered everywhere.

It is important not to sweat the small stuff when you are with kinesthetics. **The more casual you are, the better they like it.** Touch is extremely important to them, and they will touch you as well, hugging freely or holding hands. They don't mind public displays of affection, and will give this freely too. Wear soft, touchable clothing when you are with them. Kinesthetics like just about anything that involves the body. A good gift for a kinesthetic would be anything that is comfortable on her body, or an ice cream cone regu-larly in the evening, her favorite food, an afternoon doing her favorite sport, or a day at the beach if she loves the water. **Anything personal means a lot to the kinesthetic, like little thoughtful notes, or remembering special oc-casions and anything that stimulates her skin.** If she likes the cologne you wear, always wear it. If she likes the way you smell after you exercise (no kidding!), then don't shower.

It is important to tell a kinesthetic how you feel about her and to touch and hold her as much as possible. Physical affection is what she thrives on and is the key to her heart. Don't confuse this with sex, but instead understand that the realm of the emotions is always linked physically to her body. Feelings, which to a kinesthetic are comprised of a <u>physical</u> and an <u>emotional</u> element will be what eventually bonds her to you and will be eventually why she will want to make love to you. She is highly intuitive and also has a strong B.S. detector so any kind of false praise or moves meant to try to maneuver her into bed will be seen through. **The more <u>genuine</u> you are with her, the more she will be drawn to you.**

Matching predicates, mirroring body language and accepting the lifestyle of the person you are attracted to is extremely important. You do not have to become like her, but being in sync with her, appearing to have similar interests and dreams is extremely important to sexual chemistry. NLP is a map that will teach you the foreign language of the one you love. Practice matching her predicates and getting into her world; she will love you even more.

We like people who are like us, who behave in ways which match the way we see ourselves. So if you find yourself attracted to your opposite, learn that your differences can be wonderful and expand your horizons. What causes many a breakup is that we try to change our lovers so that they will be more like us, when what we were attracted to in the first place was that they had qualities we didn't have!

**"You never know a man until you
walk a mile in his moccasins."**
—Ancient Native American Saying

HOW TO GET HER BACK FROM THE OTHER GUY

First of all, if you really want to get her back, you need to decide if you want her the way she is <u>now</u>, flaws and all. If you're thinking that she's going to change, you're in for a lot of pain, and even if she does come back, you two may break up again. So, if you've decided that you can accept her the way she is and that you really want to try this, here's the way to do it. No guarantees, but if you play it right, you might pull it off.

If you two have had a relationship for a long period of time, and if she left you, the odds are very good that you might have a chance. Here's why. The deep roots of your relationship are still in the soil. Now, while the breakup may still be hopefully fresh, before she puts down roots with the new man she's with, she still feels bonded to you, although granted, she may be trying to break those bonds. It is very difficult to pull yourself out of a relationship and plant yourself in a new pot. Even if she does manage to pull herself away from you, she won't have any new roots to hold her in her new relationship and stabilize her for a long time.

What you have going in your favor are the roots that are still in that soil; the time, love, energy and commitment that you both put into this relationship. It will be exceedingly hard for her to forget the love you shared together. And that is the love that you'll use to win her back. If, that is, you are willing to change. Yes, you heard that right. Because, I'm assuming that she left you for what was, to her, a good reason. When the hard times set in with her new lover, as they always do, <u>be consistently friendly and supportive</u>. Tell her that you understand how you hurt her or didn't give her what she needed—it is possible that you can start again. If you have had a long relationship with her, you have a very good chance of starting over because the <u>consistency</u> and <u>emotional support</u> you are giving her will outweigh the struggles of going through it again with someone new. In addition, <u>you know now what not to do,</u> if you play your cards right.

What's a good enough reason for a woman to leave a man? Well, to name a few:

"A" Crimes:

1. A tendency to work all the time and never give her the attention that she needs.
2. A selfish nature—it was always your needs first, rarely hers.
3. An inability to provide for her or the family financially.
4. Refusing to help with the housework.
5. An inability to talk about your feelings.
6. Not spending enough time with the children.

"B" Crimes:

1. An affair or several.
2. Verbal or physical abuse toward her or your children.
3. Gambling.
4. Drinking or drug use.
5. Dangerous or illegal activities that would put her in jeopardy.

If you are guilty of "A" list crimes, your job will be hard, but not impossible. With some will power and effort you can change those habits so that if she returns, she will be getting what she wants.

If, on the other hand, you are guilty of "B" list crimes, I'm wondering if you are really serious about changing.

Fact: 80 percent of all alcoholics return to drinking even after going through rehabilitation.

So, if your problem is your drinking, how many times has she left you before? If this is not the first time she's left, you may be out of luck. It will be a extremely difficult for her to justify going back to you if you didn't change the last time she came back. Some drug habits are easier to kick than alcohol, it all depends on your will power, and how much you really want to help yourself. It also depends on how badly you hurt her. If physical or verbal abuse was involved, you may not win her back, but you now have the chance to start over, *if you've really hit bottom.* How much more do you have to lose before you decide to change?

If you've been caught in an affair, and you don't have a <u>regular</u> pattern of lying and running off with other women, chances are good that she'll take you back. Studies show that over time wives soften when the man seriously says he will change. And she believes him, that is. But if you are used to doing this kind of thing, if you are merely trying to do damage control, you'll return to your old behavior when things get difficult again.

The reason you are having affairs is sort of predestined by biology; men do roam more than women because it's the male's function to carry on the species. Having more than one partner is common for good looking, charismatic, genetically advantaged jerks. But remember, just because it is biological doesn't mean that it's the way it *should* be, or that are you are helplessly at the whim of your genetic predisposition. "Mr. Happy" is a lame excuse! **As thinking animals, we have the power to chose the higher ground.**

Again, it all depends on what it's worth to you. If it's not worth some deep soul searching, counseling, looking yourself in the eye and taking inventory, then you probably will spend your life going from one flower to another. But if you want a true partner, a mate by your side, someone who cares if you live or die, you'll have to be faithful.

If you were verbally or physically abusive to your family, if you were violent, you will need counseling and it's going to take a long time. Do you have what it takes? Most don't. The reason you became so unhappy and lashed out at her is because of your constitution and the things that hurt you in your past. You have been treating others as you have been treated. You will need to heal yourself and learn new habits.

Back to the lists, most of the crimes on the "A" list can be changed with some will power and maybe some sessions with a counselor who can help suggest some strategies, (see Chapter Twelve.) These crimes indicate that you are paying too little attention to what's around you and too much attention to yourself. You have become self-absorbed and selfish. If you want her back, learn to give and then you will get.

People become stingy and withhold when they have been wounded. Sometimes it becomes a vicious cycle. You feel like you have so little left to give, so you keep to yourself and nobody gets a chance to help you fill up the emptiness inside you. Learn to give for the joy of giving, then others will give back to you...and learn to do dishes too!

In Chapter Six I discussed how to talk more with your mate and share your feelings. One of the primary needs a woman has is that of feeling emotionally nurtured. The main way a woman feels good in her relationship is to believe the man really cares about what she is saying, and is not just tolerating her requests for intimacy.

OK, OK, you want to know how to get her back; you think all that stuff I just said is philosophy. Well, you'll be history if you can't show her <u>before she takes you back</u> that you HAVE changed, that you ARE going to give her what she needs.

What if you don't know what she needs or why she left you? I seriously doubt that, before she left you, she didn't tell you <u>over and over again</u> what she wanted. But, it is possible that you have a quiet mouse on your hands, in which case you will need to ask her. Call her up and tell her that you want to have coffee with her. If she refuses, find some reason like returning some of her belongings, anything, just get ten minutes with her.

In those ten minutes, I want you to ask her, in a polite, HUMBLE way what it was that made her leave. AND LISTEN TO EVERY WORD SHE SAYS. I mean zip the lip! If you want her back, you absolutely have to do this. Don't interrupt and say yes, but <u>you</u> did blah, blah, blah. . . . That's not the point here.

I am <u>not</u> saying that she didn't have a part in the fighting, that she didn't <u>contribute</u> whatever finally sent her packing, but you want her to see the *changed* you, and the changed you LISTENS. If you've been a doormat, she's likely going to be really sweet and tell you that she doesn't feel THAT way about you. **(LJBF'd again!)** When she does, ask her to get specific about her complaints. She wanted <u>you</u> to have plans, <u>you</u> to decide where you were going for dinner, <u>you</u> to be more passionate? Great! Now you've got some concrete things to do.

She's not going to take you back right away. No way. But, armed with the knowledge of what she wants, you are going to set siege to her resistance and out wait her. You are going to court her, climb the walls of her fortress and simply insist on her taking you back after you do all the things she wants. You are going to *show* her by example that you are a changed man. . . Way!

If you think that perhaps this is all too humiliating, especially when she had a part in it and that no man ever begs— WRONG! The good salesman, when he loses a sale, will sometimes go back to the client he lost, ask why he lost the sale, and then try to win back the business. Well, now you're in the love business. And believe me, if she is starting to date someone new, you have some fierce competition, because HE'S on his best behavior. That's why this is a game of strategy and master cool.

About him, let's face it. He has something that you weren't giving her and that's why she is with him now instead of you. Maybe she's just out for his money, which is something you can't do much about overnight, in which case I say you are better off without her. But more likely, **she chose some-one who gives her what she feels she desperately needs.** She needed it enough to go to him, to give up on what you both had together. So, isn't that trait that you're missing important to learn? What's on your side is that after a few months have gone by he's going to be showing his dirty underwear and she will slowly see that he isn't all that she thought he was. Maybe she did make the wrong decision, she wonders. If you're not a changed man when she figures this out you don't stand a chance. Just when she feels like coming home you'll blow up and do something stupid and ruin it. Cool, think cool.

That's why seeing her regularly and persistently with your new habits over the period of time that she is with him will only make you look better and better. **Remember, what you have going for you is all those good times you had together and you need to be reminding her of them.** Tell her you want to be her friend, (this time, being a friend works!) and that anytime she wants to call you up if she's having problems you will be there for her. Offer to fix her car or to paint the porch. Be in her life as much as you can be without wearing out your welcome. Do not play hard to get; do not allow yourself to get angry and pull at her and insist that she come back. Do tell her in a level, direct voice that you want her back if she will only give you the chance. No begging, just straightforward. When she says no, tell her that you are willing to wait; smile and say that she's worth it! If she wants to cry on your shoulder when things go badly with what's-his-name, don't leap in immediately and try to seduce her, let her "have her feelings." She really does want you to be her friend now! And maybe that's something you weren't able to be before, when you didn't have time for her because you were so busy being a jerk.

If you were more passive and let her push you around, make sure that you act as confident as possible when you visit her. Spruce yourself up, get some new clothes and get rid of that plastic calculator watch she hated. Think lean and mean. Lose weight and lift weights. Be aggressive. Show up spontaneously and ask to take her out to dinner. This is something you probably never did before. Talk in a direct manner and cut out the wishy-washy stuff! He who hesitates is lost. **She wouldn't have stayed with you all that time if you didn't have some spectacular qualities.** Now, you're just going to add the traits you haven't practiced before. When Jon was trying to get me back, he finally started being willing to be outdoors, something I loved that wasn't really his thing; (I was a kinesthetic, he was a visual.) He did everything that I had always asked him to do when we were together! And it worked.

Meanwhile, you are doing lots of little things to smuggle yourself under the walls of her defense. You are leaving her favorite cookies in her mailbox; you are leaving her a note on her car. You call her answering service during the day and sing "your" favorite song.

Remember what her primary mode is (visual, auditory or kinesthetic, see Chapter Ten—NLP.) Make sure that you do things that fit with her mode. Leave voice messages for the auditory, warm mittens for the kinesthetic, a postcard of Portland for the visual. Be persistent but not obnoxious. When she asks you to leave, you leave with a smile on your face. You will not let her see you sweat! Think General Patton! I suggest for the first two months that you try to see her at the least twice a week; but you shouldn't be lurking in her driveway when she comes home. Always make a date to see her and be willing to accept what you can get. Treat her like a friend, and she won't feel so suspicious. When she accuses you of trying to get back together you sigh and say that it's so difficult because you love her so much. Then you say in a level voice, "So how <u>are</u> things going with what's-his-name." And you listen.

When they have a falling out, you'll be there to console her. You tell her that you'll go over and KILL the bastard if he hurts her. Be her knight! Be her rock. And when the time is right, and she lets you put your arms around her and hold her, look at her and tell her that you want her back and that if she'll only give the relationship a chance, you'd be the happiest man in the world. If you were together for over a year and you didn't propose, seriously consider it NOW. You can talk about what you want from the relationship after the dust has settled. She may come back to you when her new relationship hits the rocky road, and she may not.

You need to be continuously evaluating yourself for signs of self-abuse. Doing all this stuff will not make you look weak if you are doing it out of sincere, gutsy love for her, and you are not collapsing under all your guilt and beating yourself up for the mistakes you made. That's all in the past. **If you're acting like poor little please love me, no of course she's not going to go back to you.** In the first stages, she will need to vent at you. That's OK. <u>She needs to do that to get close to you again</u>, so listen to her patiently. But if it goes on and on, you've got the wrong girl.

And if she doesn't take you back, what you have built for yourself is a sense of pride and drive, and that is very sexy to a lot of OTHER women. If she hasn't decided whether to take you back or not, and she's waffling, this is when you let it slip (because you are friends, of course, and would she mind listening to you?) that you have this other woman in your life and can't decide whether to go for it or not. Then— disappear for awhile. This maneuver is <u>intermittent reinforcement</u> at its best. You make her wonder what you've been up to. You make her miss you. The showdown is coming; you can't go on like this forever.

When and if she starts showing you non-verbal signs of affection, when she starts leaning on you, and especially when she starts letting you kiss her, then you need to have—a TALK!

Even if she hasn't started being affectionate, you need to pick an arbitrary cutoff point for this courtship beyond which you won't suffer.

Do this in the beginning to keep yourself sane. Let's say, in three months you'll know that either you have her or you WILL move on. At about two months, tell her that you love her but you can't wait forever for her, if she is going to come back to you, you need to know pretty soon. Let her know again that the other women are NOTHING like her, (but they sure are there!) And you *should* be dating other women while this is going on to keep things in perspective. After you tell her you can't wait much longer, disappear and call her in a week. Then, **ask her what it is that she needs to have from you to make her feel safe.** This is REALLY important. If it's a promise that you'll never work weekends again, give it to her; if she wants you to lose weight, she should already see that you have lost ten! In other words, she should have very little to complain about but the past!

Now, all you need is a little sugar. . . .

This is the very last, last thing that you're going to do to win her back, and it had better be a doozie as they used to say. One of my boyfriends flew us to Disney World to try to win me over, and another one took me to a B&B for a surprise weekend. **But you don't need money to win her if she really wants to come back, you just need a show of heart and guts.** Think of something she's always wanted to do or have. Take her water rafting or buy her that car. Propose to her if you've decided that's what it'll take. Do it with all your heart and soul and don't hold back. It's all up to the gods at this point.

You want to walk away knowing that you did everything that you could to get what you wanted.

. . . . Most importantly, it will be for your own self-esteem that you did it. You learned new habits, you changed your selfish ways and you took a big risk to do it. You did it to prove to her, but more importantly to prove to yourself that you *are* a winner and that you *do* deserve the best!

And if she can't appreciate you after all you went through for her, believe me, a woman who is even better is waiting for you right now.

"For most people, the fantasy is driving around in a big car having all the chicks you want, and being able to pay for it. It has always been, still is, and always will be. Anyone who says it isn't, is talking bullshit."

—Mick Jagger

Some people sit on
their butts,

Got the dream but not
the guts

That's peachy for
some people

For some hum-drum
people you see

But some people
ain't me

—*Mama Rose* from *Gypsy*

Getting 12 Yourself To Do It

'm going to dispense with motivational pep talks and the theoretical jargon as much as I can in this chapter. You've read most of it somewhere else anyway. The bottom line is this:

Either you want to change your habits and find a way to get yourself to do this or you don't.

Change is a bitch and it's definitely female.

I'd like to prove my point. Look up from where you are sitting right now. Now think of three things about your love life you have been putting off; things that would make you feel better if you did them.

Have your three things? OK. Now, put down this book, go get a piece of paper and <u>write down the steps you'll need to take to get one of those things done</u> . . .Ready?

GO!

OK, now you've turned the page. Did you go and make your list?

Of course not! Instead, you turned the page because you're no dummy; you think, what's this woman up to?

Well, I'll give you another chance. Use the blank space here to make your list.

Some suggestions:

- practice talking to women
- call up Ingrid and ask her to marry you
- get better clothes
- lose weight
- start lifting at the gym
- ask Fred at work for Karen's phone number
- put in a personal ad
- join a tennis club

The odds are 90% that you didn't do the exercise. Most people are lazy and resist change.

- What if I told you that if you don't start doing some of the things that I suggest, the odds on you changing your sex life are next to none?

- What if I told you that:

  If you don't find a wife or a steady girlfriend; if you live without physical affection, you will die of heart illness or loneliness much sooner than a guy who is married? It's a Fact!

- **What if you knew that your penis would fall off in one week unless you started taking some action?**

If that last little item were true ALL of you would be doing the things I suggest...you just have to want it bad enough...Let's try something else. Read this exercise first, then close your eyes and do it:

I want you to see yourself on your death bed. Imagine what that would be like. Now tell yourself what you would have done differently if you had your life to live over again.

I hope that had an effect. Those of you who really want to change your love life will get up, get a pencil, turn back the page and do your list of three things. . . .

OK. You did it? Great! Now here are some ways to get yourself to do the things on your list.

1. <u>Set a time goal</u> for each of your items and break each item down into manageable steps. By next Tuesday, you'll ask Rebecca out. By next Friday, you'll work out three times, whatever.

2. <u>Give yourself a reward</u> when you get your task done. You get to go rollerblading! You get to go out to dinner.

3. <u>Tell yourself that, until you do what you've planned to do, you don't get to do something that you love.</u> This is the old "no TV until after you do your homework" trick.

You like to eat ice cream? Then you don't get to have any until you go out to three places looking for women (if you decided that was a step on the way to your goal of having a girlfriend.)

4. <u>Call up one of your friends and tell them your goal</u>. Tell them you'll pay them a certain amount of money if you don't meet your goal. The more it hurts, the better. This social pressure works great. If you don't have anyone to help motivate you, it will be harder. You can use me. Write me a letter telling me what you plan to do and when you plan on doing it. Then if you don't meet your goal, you will send me $100 which I'll send to the charity of my choice. You could also send a blank check to your mother or sister telling them that they can fill it in by a certain date unless you get something done you've been meaning to do. Lie if you're too embarrassed to tell them what it is.

5. <u>Make a big monthly chart</u> and mark off steps or goals that you will do on certain days. Or stick a sign on your shaving mirror that reads: **Only 40 more days until my fortieth birthday.**

6. <u>Eliminate sources of distraction.</u> One guy I worked with watched TV all the time. This was his big excuse for not dating. I told him to unplug it and turn off the cable. I told another guy to turn his sofa upside down when he said it was hard for him to stop being a coach potato. (I turned my TV off three years ago. Entire series have gone by and I didn't watch them. I don't miss it. I've gained time.)

7. <u>Flood yourself with what you are avoiding.</u>

- This is a very important tool. It's the way I got myself to start dating when I was stuck. It takes a lot of guts to do it. But boy, does it work and it works fast. **To "flood" yourself means to expose yourself to what you are afraid of until you aren't afraid of it anymore.** You're afraid of elevators? You go up and down in one all day.

- So, you haven't been getting out around women because you're afraid of getting rejected? Well, that's what you go out to do. Tell yourself that you will talk with thirty women in one week. **Thirty** you say? How can I do that? Well, you look for events in the newspaper that probably will draw a lot of people and then you go there and talk with the women. Or you go to a **meet market** on Friday night. You count 1-2-3.

As you start out:

- Your anxiety will rise.

- You might feel like you are going to pass out.

- You might be viciously attacked by awful thoughts about yourself. Grrrrrrrr

- But you don't stop! You are going to do this because you need to learn to talk to women before you can get dates, so you keep doing it.

That's the ticket. As you get to higher and higher numbers of women, you may soon feel like running and getting the hell out of there. **It is extremely important that you stay there and continue with the exercise at that point.** If you quit and leave, you will be <u>reinforcing your avoidance</u>.

It will feel so good to get out of there. . . . You'll think I am nuts for asking you to do that and that you did the right thing. You go home, pop open a cold one and BOY DOES THAT TASTE GOOD.

You have appeased yourself with a temporary feel good. The problem with a temporary feel good is that:

You are not seeing the long term consequences of avoiding doing what will, in the long run, be better for you.

- **In the moment** those French fries will taste great. But if you need to lose weight, and the fat will cause your cholesterol to go higher, putting you in danger of having a heart attack, it's not helping.

- **In the moment** that cigarette tastes great, but how many people died of lung cancer one cigarette at a time? How many people were killed on the highway by someone who became an alcoholic one drink at a time?

Back to "flooding" yourself to get over your fear. Don't run when your anxiety begins to rise. Stay there in that bar or at that party and keep going. At some point, when you have completely immersed yourself in this exercise, <u>you will feel yourself take off.</u> You will start to have fun; you will start to relax. You'll suddenly notice that *you aren't nervous anymore,* you'll look at the girl you're talking to and think: *she is just another woman.* **If she doesn't like me, there will be other women.**

The chart below gives a picture of how to "flood" yourself.

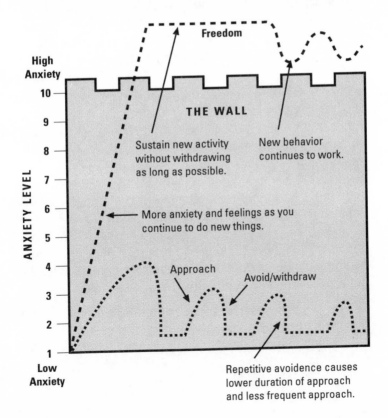

Babe Ruth used to smile every time he struck out. The press asked him why he was smiling. He said, "Because I know I'm that much closer to hitting a home run."

In order to succeed double your failure rate.
Thomas Watson

- It's a numbers game. Think quantity.

- If you don't want to set a number count, set a time limit: You will ask women to dance for at least two hours. You will not stop until the time is up. Use this technique for anything you've been avoiding. You will work for two hours, then you get to quit and lay in the sun. You will exercise for one hour, then you get to watch TV.

- So set your goal and count—just count. <u>Flooding</u> is the shortest and the fastest way to get over your resistance to something. It's the difference between taking the Bandaide off slowly or rapidly.

8. <u>Visualize.</u> There are lots of ways to do this. When I got really nervous at a dance, while I was trying to meet guys almost ten years ago, I did this. I wanted men to ask me to dance. "Who is popular?" I thought. Of course! And so, I imagined I was the prom queen. **Acting as if** I was her allowed me to feel that I could smile at anyone. Everyone loved me—I imagined everyone thought I was special. And I was projecting happy energy, <u>so it worked!</u> Imagining myself as a more confident person, someone I could picture in my mind, walking like them, talking like them, turned my nervous "date hunts" into exciting safaris! **Act as if** you are a Roman conqueror, a LARGE Roman conqueror. You can be the president; You can be Clint Eastwood.

Or you can act like a dweeb and sit at home alone another night having virtual sex.

9. Self-talk. Have you ever used this? Or, have you been taught this and never used it? Try this one: Say to yourself:

Women are wonderful

Sex is wonderful and

I am wonderful.

When the negative thoughts rush in, replace them with that, or make up your own. And remember our old phrase:

It's not whether I'm good enough for her

It's whether she's good enough for me

10. Kinesthetic Reminders. These are little ways you remind yourself of your goals on a daily basis. I call them kinesthetic because you put them somewhere on your body. The most common trick is a rubber band around your wrist. I have a toe ring I wear to remind me to MOVE FORWARD in my goals. Others:

Take your watch off the wrist you usually wear it on and put it on the other one; every time you look at the time, you'll be reminded of your goal.

Buy a vibrating pager you can set to remind yourself of your goal. It goes off silently, and works great. See the MotivAider in the *Resource Section*.

Put a quarter in your shoe; change it to the other shoe weekly. I'm sure you can think of others.

WAYS TO REDUCE YOUR ANXIETY

The more you avoid doing what you want to do the more anxiety you will experience. And when you do start doing what you want to do, the more feelings (that you may label anxiety) you will have. This is because you are expanding your consciousness through risk. Learn to use anxiety as a positive force. When you feel your stomach go off, it means that you need to take care of yourself by doing things that'll get you what you want.

Anxiety is the body's alarm clock.
It says wake up!

Here Are Some Ways To Reduce Your Anxiety Until You Take Action:

White light

Imagine that you are covered by a soothing white light. It starts a little above your head and comes down over your face, shoulders, arms, chest, back, hips, legs, over your entire body like water and under your feet and around your back just like a cocoon. This white, warm light can protect you when you feel distress. Imagine that you are covered with this light before you go into situations that you fear. If your girlfriend is bugging you, surround yourself with this light, sit in it and listen to her. Or, imagine throwing the light around the two of you so that you are both in the cocoon together. It's amazing how people calm down when you do this. Breathe this light in. You will feel much better. Some say this is the light of God or the universe. It is <u>always</u> there and it <u>will</u> help you.

The amazing inverted black triangle

I have no idea how this works, but it does. (Do you always have to know how something works?) This is another visualization tool. When you feel anger coming toward you, or a verbal assault of some kind, imagine throwing this inverted black triangle between you and the negative source. Leave it there and you'll notice a change in the energy. You can do this when you're on the phone or in person. Just let it block out the bad energy and you'll be protected.

When you are scared

Imagine yourself as a small child, perhaps somewhere between five and twelve years old. Now, as your adult self, take yourself as a young child by the hand and talk gently to yourself. Tell your child self that no one will hurt you, and that you're going to be there to protect him. Sit little you next to big you and explain what's happening to him when he gets scared. Or imagine your adult self stepping in front of your child self when he gets threatened. Be there for him because if you aren't there he will get hurt. . . .And YOU are really the only one who can be a parent to him now.

Breathing

Lay down on the floor. Breathe in and out to the count of ten. Put your hand on your heart to soothe yourself. Deep breathing is very calming.

Exercise

You know it makes you feel better. And it beats therapy bills or sick days.

Medicine

If your anxiety never seems to end, I suggest that you see an M.D. and discuss a trial of the medicine *Xanax* or *Ativan*—two anti-anxiety drugs that are safe in small dosages. Did you know that some doctors have been sued for NOT prescribing these medicines? They let their patients go on feeling terrible when they could have helped them considerably with a temporary prescription. So much of what we feel emotionally is caused by temporary chemical imbalances in our nervous system due to situational stress. To say that taking medicine is unnatural is like saying your car will run without gas or oil. If your body needs it, and it helps you, and you don't abuse it, there is no problem. It can also take the place of drinking too much to cut the tension when you're around women. There are natural alternatives but nothing works as rapidly to alleviate anxiety as these medicines.

ON ATTITUDE

Women are attracted to positivity and dislike a defeatist attitude. The attitude you take toward the changes in your life is clear to everyone. If you are going through financial change, experiencing divorce, or dating problems, spiritual people believe that God or your higher power is offering you a chance to change for the better through crisis. And you can create a positive outcome from all of your misfortunes. Even a divorce or heartbreak can be used as a turning point to change the course of your life. You can look at these painful occurrences as lessons that can be turned around and used to your advantage. And defeat isn't the end. It's the time to practice with a new team. To look to the new season.

I once had a client who hadn't dated in seven years. He was twenty-nine, had graduated from an ivy league school, was tall and handsome and made over sixty thousand a year. Despite all of his advantages, and perhaps in some sense because of them, he felt lousy about himself. He spent the majority of his time under a dark cloud comparing himself with other men and wondering why he was having so much trouble with women. Every time he went on a date he acted defensively, and put himself down. This became a self-fulfilling prophesy. Because he was rejected so often, he began to expect it, and behaved in ways that caused him to be rejected again. In order to break this pattern, he had to <u>make</u> himself think differently about how women treated him. He had to consciously change his thinking habits by using behavioral exercises, also known as cognitive therapy. Luckily for him, he was smart enough to get help. After he did the exercises, he had a girlfriend and was enjoying a healthy sex life within three months.

Cognitive therapy is based on the premise that it is not what happens to us that causes us to feel bad, but **what we think about what happens to us that causes our upset**. Two very good books that teach exercises to change your thought patterns are <u>Intimate Connections</u> by David Burns, M.D. and <u>Learned Optimism</u> by Martin Seligman. I strongly suggest that you buy and read them if you want to feel better.

Expect to come face to face with every negative thought you have ever had about yourself when you really begin to <u>do</u> any of the exercises in this chapter one-hundred percent. This is because you are challenging your old rigid, defense system. You **have to systematically reprogram your brain to counter self-defeating thoughts and put new ones in their place.**

SOME FINAL THOUGHTS

When a new tributary runs into a stagnant river, the water initially becomes cloudy as the mud from the bottom gets stirred up, but eventually the new river runs healthier and stronger. So, when your new actions stir up the GUNK of your bad habits, know that clear water will eventually come. Prepare for white water on the river of change. If you can ride it out, you will have smooth sailing with the moon to guide you.

And practice. Athletes try to analyze game failures so they can repeat the plays which worked and avoid the plays which didn't. The same strategy works with women. Try these techniques several ways, in different combinations, with different women. The exercises work. My clients have used them successfully for ten years. Like any new habit, they require repetition and energy. In the beginning you may not see any definite changes. You must go on faith. Like lifting weights, first you put in the effort, then you'll gradually see the results. It's unfortunate that so may false gurus, and con artists are telling people the answer is quick and easy (come to our seminar for only $500!) . . . When was the last time you learned a new, difficult skill that came easy?

In some cases, many of you have been thinking lousy things about yourself for over thirty years! You think maybe these habits are going to go away overnight? The new skills work if you work...Whose thoughts are those anyway? And whose voice is talking to you? Your father's?...your mother's? The kids at school?...Who told you that you would never be a success, maybe at *anything* let alone with women?

Well, sport, it's time to prove them wrong, if you've got the guts.

Today a client told me he would rather have his arm broken than have a girl reject him. My answer? Well, I didn't nod my head sympathetically as so many therapists had done before. And, although I am sympathetic to his pain, I said:

Well then, you'll have to decide what you want—a broken arm, or living your life without a woman—because, if you date, you are going to get rejected sometimes. The only way to avoid that is to drastically lower your standards. You are going to be disappointed, and then, after you master these new behaviors, you're going to succeed. It's part of the learning process, trial and error, what works and what doesn't. You wouldn't tell a little boy who fell off a bike trying to ride it for the first time, "Well, you might as well give up," would you? Of course not! <u>You'd teach him how to do it</u>.

Once, while skiing, I found myself on a steep hill and I was scared of falling. So I said to myself, what's the worst thing that could happen? Well, I could fall and break something. Could I live with that? I decided I could, and gave myself the room to fail, telling myself I could fall four times and I would still be doing OK. Well, I got down with only three falls, but it could just as well have been five. Giving myself room to be human helped a lot.

Go purposely into the face of fear and you'll see that fear is just an illusion, just a body sensation—adrenaline maybe, which you have labeled negatively. Any experience can be turned around if you look at it this way. You're not getting rejected—you are practicing how to talk to women, how to ask them out, you are going for your dream.

Many men give up—will you? They convince themselves that a half life without love is good enough. But, can <u>you</u> bear looking back at your life in old age, <u>seeing what you could have had if you only had taken that risk</u>? Yearning for the sea, but stuck in stagnant water? Forever seeing the mountain top but camped out safely at its foot?

Finding a woman who will love and appreciate you will be the journey of a million miles. Take it one step at a time. Now you have the map. Your courage, like the Cowardly Lion's, has always been there in your heart. One day you'll stand on the mountain top with a loving partner by your side and you will not be alone.

For *that* is what both men

and women really want.

**"Women:
Picturesque protests
against the mere
existence of
common sense."**

—*Oscar Wilde*

Resources

BOOKS

Anatomy of the Spirit Myss, Caroline. N.Y.: Harmony Books, 1996.

Are You the One for Me? DeAngelis, Barbara. N.Y.: Dell, 1992.

Awaken the Giant Within Robbins, Anthony. N.Y.: Simon & Shuster, 1992.

Feeling Good Burns, David. N. Y.: Morrow, 1980.

For Each Other Barbach, Lonnie. N.Y.: New American Library, 1984.

Influence: The Psychology of Persuasion Cialdini, Robert. N.Y.: William Morrow, 1983.

Instant Rapport Brooks, Michael. N.Y.: Warner Books, 1989.

Intimate Connections Burns, David. N.Y.: Penguin Books, 1980.

Learned Optimism Seligman, Martin. N. Y.: Kompft, 1990.

Letting Go Cabot, Tracy & Wanderer, Zev. N.Y.: Bantam, 1978.

Living in the Light & **Creative Visualization** (two separate books) Gawain, Shakt. San Rafael: New World Library, 1986.

Sex, A Man's Guide Bechtel, Steven and Stains. Penn.: Rodale, 1996.

The Evolution of Desire Buss, David. N.Y: Basic Books, 1995.

The New Male Sexuality Zilbergeld, Bernie Banton Books: New York, 1993.

ANTHROPOLOGICAL STUDIES
CONCERNING MATING BEHAVIOR

Berscheid, E. & Dion, K. (1971). Physical attractiveness and dating choice. Journal of Experimental and Social Psychology, 7.

Berscheid, E. & Walster, E. (1972). What is beautiful is good. Journal of Personality and Social Psychology, 24.

Darwin, C. (1871). The Descent of Man and Selection in Relation to Sex, London: John Murray.

Davis, Simon (1990). Men as success objects and women as sex objects: A study of personal advertisements. Sex Roles.

Givens, D. (1978). The non-verbal basis of attraction: Flirtation, courtship, and seduction. Psychiatry. Hager, J. C. & Ekman, P. (1979). Long distance transmission of facial affect signals. Ethology and Sociobiology.

Mead, M (1967). Male and Female: A study of the sexes in a changing world. New York: William Morrow.

Mueser, K., Grau, B., Sussman, S., & Rosen, A. (1984) You're only as pretty as you feel: Facial expression as determinant of physical attractiveness. Journal of Personality and Social Psychology, 46.

Riggio, R. & Woll, S. (1984). The role of non-verbal cues and physical attractiveness in the selection of dating partners. Journal of Social and Personal Relationships, 1.

Scheflen, A. E. (1964) The significance of posture in communication systems. Psychiatry, 27.

Stake, J. & Lauer, M. (1987). The consequences of being overweight: A controlled study of gender differences, Sex Roles, 17.

Symons, D. (1979). Evolution of human sexuality. New York: Oxford Press.

Townsend, J. M. & Levy, G. D. (1990). Effects of potential partners' physical attractiveness and socio-economic status on sexuality and partner selection. Journal of Psychology, 124.

VIDEO, CATALOGUES, MISCELLANEOUS ITEMS

Blowfish. Catalogues, erotic books, toys, videos. 2261 Market St. #284, San Francisco, Ca. 94114. 415-864-0880. E-mail: blowfish@netcom.com

Good Vibrations. Sells vibrators, lubricants, sexual toys, and other goodies. 800-289-8423. E-mail: goodvibe@well.sf.ca.us

Better Sex Video Series. Three tapes are helpful: "Better Sex Basics," "Advanced Sexual Techniques," "Sex Games and Toys." 800-888-1900

Catalogue: Focus International Titles: "Erections" (about causes and treatment for problems), "You Can Last Longer" (a demonstration of the "stop-start" and "squeeze" techniques). 800-843-0305

MotivAider. A great tool. A conditioning buzzer which you can clip to your belt. It vibrates silently and reminds you of your goals. 800-456-9887

Shoes with invisible lifts. Used by commodity brokers to look taller: Mason Shoes, Chippewa Falls, Wi. 800-826-7030

Plastic surgery for men: Dr. James Billie. Board Certified Plastic Surgeon. Located in Little Rock, Arkansas (and thus much more reasonable than prices elsewhere): 800-877-7926. It'll be the best decision you ever made. Dr. Billie is phenomenally good, and does very natural work. Call Susan Clark at his office for more information.

BOOKS TO ORDER

These books are available directly from **Island Flower Books**. See the order blank in the back.

Nice Guys Don't Get Laid by Marcus Meleton. This book is very funny and some of the material is right on. The rest of it should be taken as is - humor. It contains cartoons about doormat-related problems with women. The author gives even more evidence why you shouldn't be a doormat. All the men who read it like it and refer it on their friends. Meleton is a recovering "nice guy". $10.00

Bald Men Always Come Out On Top. Beswick, Dave St. Augustin: Ama Publishing. A funny book. It's a combination of humor, advice and honest communication for bald men and those who love them written by a bald author. Contains cartoons and anecdotes. It's a great gift. $13.00

43 Thing To Do Besides Go To A Bar. A 10 page pamphlet listing specific ideas for looking for women by Dr. Clark. $5.00

How to Meet and Date Younger Women by Dr Clark. A 20 page pamphlet which gives details: Where they go and how to successfully attract them. $10.00

PRIVATE CONSULTATIONS WITH DR. JAMA CLARK

Dr. Clark is available for private consultations by phone nationally or in person in San Francisco and Sacramento, California. Most men have individual questions about the problems they are having with women. To answer your specific questions, it is necessary to ask you about your "history," or the background to your problem. This could include, but is not limited to asking you about your dating history, childhood illnesses, schooling, marital history, fathering history as well as the way your parents interacted with you during childhood. The reason this is necessary is that you are unique and many things may have happened to you to cause your current situation. Your problems did not appear out of thin air!

What you will get from this consultation:

1. REASONS FOR YOUR PROBLEM—As succinctly as possible, you will learn some reasons you may be having this problem. The longer Dr. Clark talks with you, the more specific her feedback will become. Obviously, in a one and one half hour session, it will be impossible to learn ALL of your personal background. However, you will learn the general origin of your problem

2. SOLUTIONS—You will receive specific, behavioral suggestions about how to go about understanding and changing

your problem. This could include, but is not limited to things to do such as:

■ Why the woman you are with is doing what she is doing and how to handle it ■ The best way to meet better looking women ■ Spiritual answers to concrete problems ■ Other helpful aides to anxiety such as visualization, meditation and individualized programs geared to your specific problem ■ Referrals to physicians that can help you with medical problems ■ How to reduce your anxiety with women ■ Feedback on your personal appearance. Please send a picture to *Island Flower Books* before your consultation date. Allow one week. Videos are very helpful. ■ Help to get you back out on the dating scene, to break through procrastination after divorce or heartbreak.

3. DIRECT AND TO THE POINT—Dr. Clark is known for her honesty. Please understand that in order to help you with your problem, she may need to ask you personal questions that may be embarrassing. Questions about your sexual habits, dating habits and addictive habits are quite common. Should you wish to talk to other men who have consulted with Dr. Clark, she will be glad to give you the numbers of many men who have benefited from her help.

How To Schedule: For phone consultations, call *Island Flower Books* (800 - BOOKS-41). Leave the best time to contact you, and what times are best for your consultation. Include your area code. Dr. Clark will set up appointments with you. You will need to pay for the appointment call, and give prepayment with a credit card. Initial appointments must be one and one half hours in length in order to take a background of your problem.

Fees: Initial consultation: $ 110 for 1 1/2 hours. Additional hours are billed at $85 dollars an hour. Fees are subject to change after December 31, 1997.

"Here's to Woman!
Would that we
could fall
into her arms
without falling
into her hands."

—*Ambrose Bierce*

Index

Taxes: All taxes are included in the book price

Shipping: OVERNIGHT SHIPPING/HANDLING add $5.00 for each copy of *What The Hell DO Women Really Want?* (hardback). Add $3.00 for other books (softback).

Regular Mail: add $2.00 PER ITEM to the total cost (book rate orders take 4-5 weeks)

UPS: Add $ 3.00 For the first item, Add $1.50 for each additional item

Payment: Check (checks payable to *Island Flower Books*) VISA, MASTER CARD (no Discover, Am Express, Optima) and money order.

Card Number: _____Exp. Date_____

ORDER FORM

WHAT THE HELL DO WOMEN REALLY WANT? is available directly from *Island Flower Books* through the following methods:

Phone Orders: Toll free: 1-800-BOOKS-41 (1-800-266-5741). Please have your credit card ready.

Fax Orders: 1-415-951-1954

Mail Orders: Island Flower Books
P.O. Box 472157
San Francisco, CA 94147-2157

E-mail orders: www.dr.clark.com

	Item	Price	Amount
_____	What the Hell Do Women Really Want?	$22.95	_____
_____	Bald Men Always Come Out on Top	$13.00	_____
_____	Nice Guys Don't Get Laid	$10.00	_____
_____	43 things to Do Besides Go To A Bar	$ 5.00	_____
_____	How To Meet and Date Younger Women	$10.00	_____
		SUBTOTAL	_____

Add Shipping Costs (see other side): _____

TOTAL _____

Taxes: All taxes are included in the book price

Shipping: OVERNIGHT SHIPPING/HANDLING add $5.00 for each copy of *What The Hell DO Women Really Want?* (hardback). Add $3.00 for other books (softback).

Regular Mail: add $2.00 PER ITEM to the total cost (book rate orders take 4-5 weeks)

UPS: Add $ 3.00 For the first item, Add $1.50 for each additional item

Payment: Check (checks payable to *Island Flower Books*) VISA, MASTER CARD (no Discover, Am Express, Optima) and money order.

Card Number: _____Exp. Date_____

ORDER FORM

WHAT THE HELL DO WOMEN REALLY WANT? is available directly from *Island Flower Books* through the following methods:

Phone Orders: Toll free: 1-800-BOOKS-41 (1-800-266-5741). Please have your credit card ready.

Fax Orders: 1-415-951-1954

Mail Orders: Island Flower Books
P.O. Box 472157
San Francisco, CA 94147-2157

E-mail orders: www.dr.clark.com

	Item	Price	Amount
_____	What the Hell Do Women Really Want?	$22.95	_____
_____	Bald Men Always Come Out on Top	$13.00	_____
_____	Nice Guys Don't Get Laid	$10.00	_____
_____	43 things to Do Besides Go To A Bar	$ 5.00	_____
_____	How To Meet and Date Younger Women	$10.00	_____
		SUBTOTAL	_____

Add Shipping Costs (see other side): _____

TOTAL _____